S0-BZG-628

First Aid

First Aid

What to do and When

John Books

MEDICAL CONSULTANT

J. MERVYN LLOYD M.D.

GOLDEN APPLE PUBLISHERS

The information and recommendations contained in this book are intended to complement, not substitute for, the advice of your own physician. Before starting any medical treatment, exercise program or diet, consult your physician. Information in this book is given without any guarantees on the part of the author, Footnote Productions Limited, The Quarto Group Inc. or Golden Apple Publishers and they cannot be held responsible for the contents in this book.

First Aid

A Golden Apple Publication
Published by arrangement with
Footnote Productions Limited
A Division of the Quarto Group, Inc.

June 1987

Golden Apple is a trademark of
Golden Apple Publishers

All rights reserved.
Copyright © 1987 by the Quarto Group, Inc.

This book may not be reproduced, in whole or in part by mimeograph or any other means without permission. For information, address: Golden Apple Publishers, 666 Fifth Avenue, New York 10103.

Printed in Hong Kong

9 8 7 6 5 4 3 2 1

ISBN 0-553-19916-1

CONTENTS

INTRODUCTION

First aid is just that—the *first* aid given to someone who has been injured or become ill. Since most accidents happen around the home, it's important for you to know how and what steps to take before medical help is available. By learning basic first aid, you can offer immediate treatment, and your apparent confidence will soothe the injured person.

Your first job as a first-aider is to decide the urgency of the situation. Sometimes you will have to act quickly to save a life. At other times, your duties will be to avoid further injury and get additional help. Whatever you are required to do, your first job is to take action. If there are other people around, ask them to call an ambulance or the police. If you're by yourself, make a quick decision as to the correct action and take it!

THE SIX EMERGENCY STEPS

Since it is the life-or-death situations that call for urgent actions, it is a good idea to keep in mind the six important steps of medical emergency response:

● Make sure that the victim has an open airway and is breathing. If not, open the airway and begin artificial respiration procedures.

● If the victim is bleeding, use direct pressure or a tourniquet if necessary to control it.

● Since many victims begin to panic, you should take steps to prevent further injury. Move the victim *only* if his or her present position might cause more trouble. Do not let the victim walk around. When possible keep the victim resting on the ground.

● Many serious injuries lead to the body going into shock. Look for the signs of shock and take the required first-aid actions.

● If you're not a doctor or nurse do not try to attempt things that are outside your knowledge. A wrong or improper action may lead to more serious injuries.

● Get medical help as soon as possible.

The last point is most important. Many times your mind will be racing, trying to remember all that you can do to save the victim. Often a person calls the police or the hospital and forgets to give them all the needed information. The victim may not be the *only* one to panic. Remember—when you call for help give a quick report of the situation, including where and when it happened. Before you hang up, make sure the person on the other end has all the information needed to respond. Then go back and assure the victim that help is on the way.

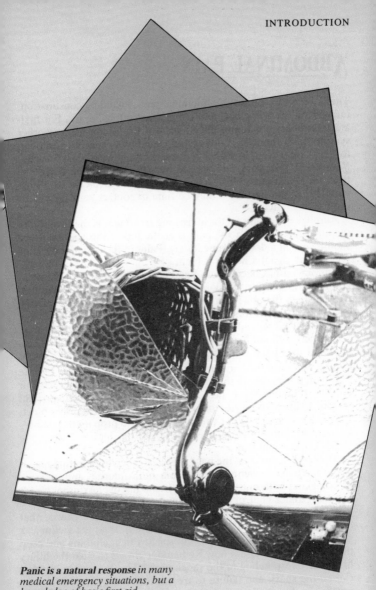

Panic is a natural response *in many medical emergency situations, but a knowledge of basic first aid procedures will help you to remain calm and take the correct decision as to what has to be done quickly.*

ABDOMINAL PAIN

There are many causes of abdominal pain, including constipation, indigestion, period pains, and cramps, as well as injury. For first-aid treatment, it is important to know if the victim has any other symptoms. If the pain is not accompanied by headache, vomiting, fever, or diarrhea it is probably not serious and won't last for long. Your local pharmacy can supply over-the-counter medicines to treat these ailments. However, as most of the medicine labels tell you, if the pain persists it may be time to contact your doctor for professional advice.

Another important factor in first-aid treatment is the location of the abdominal pain. If the pain is at the top of the abdomen you should consult a doctor immediately. Pains in the upper abdominal region may signal a heart problem.

If a person has been injured and complains of abdominal pain, you should consider the possibility of internal bleeding. Wounds that occur in the abdomen can cause severe risk to many internal organs. If the pain follows an accident or a heavy blow, or if you see some swelling and tenderness, it's time to seek medical help. Tenderness and swelling are signs of internal injuries. If you suspect that the victim has suffered an internal injury there are steps to take to reduce further damage. The first thing to do is to put the victim on the back with the knees flexed and raised with a pillow or the like. If no pillow is handy, remember that one of the important factors of any first-aid treatment is improvisation. Use any object, such as a cardboard box or rolled-up jacket, to prop up the victim's knees. The important thing is to elevate the legs and keep the victim relaxed and still.

After the victim is on the back, quickly check for external bleeding. Sometimes a victim suffers from both internal and external bleeding and both must be treated. If you discover external bleeding get it under control (see "Bleeding and Wounds").

Another possible result of internal bleeding is the chance that the victim will go into shock. As a precaution, treat the victim as a shock candidate (see "Shock"). Loosen any tight clothing and keep the victim warm, but not hot. Remember always to treat the injury first before responding to the shock possibility. It is the injury that caused the shock and failure to treat it first could result in a more severe shock reaction.

Do not give a person suffering from abdominal pain anything by mouth—it might aggravate the problem.

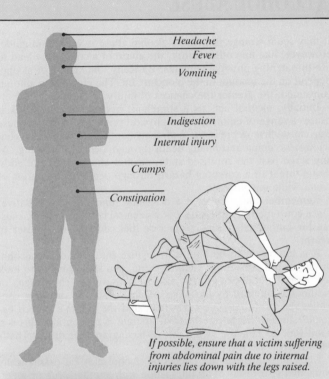

Headache
Fever
Vomiting

Indigestion
Internal injury
Cramps
Constipation

If possible, ensure that a victim suffering from abdominal pain due to internal injuries lies down with the legs raised.

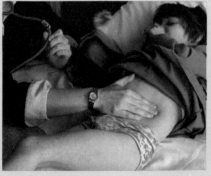

Abdominal pain is a very common childhood complaint. Your child should be examined by a doctor if the pain is severe, recurrent or prolonged.

ALCOHOL ABUSE

It may seem strange to include alcohol abuse in a first-aid guide. However, like any other injury, the abuse of alcohol may lead to life-threatening physical ailments. Basically, the effects of alcohol depend on the amount in the bloodstream. The greater the amount consumed, the greater the chances of injury.

Initially, alcohol acts as a stimulant, but as more is drunk it causes a range of emotional and physical problems. Alcohol abuse can cause first depression, and then confusion, stupor, unconsciousness, coma and finally death through alcohol poisoning. At any stage past the confused state, alcohol abuse poses the additional threat of a potential hazard through death by inhalation of vomit while unconscious.

Remember that alcohol is a drug that functions as a sedative. Once consumed, it affects the body's central nervous system, causing the emotional roller-coaster ride that can lead the abuser to death.

It is important to be able to recognize the signs of an alcohol problem. If a person has been drinking, you should begin to look for severe mood swings. An alcohol abuser may show signs of giddiness, followed by outbursts of anger. As the drinking continues the confused state takes over and the victim's speech becomes slurred. Since one facet of first aid is prevention, this is a good time to talk the victim out of having another drink. That's what friends are for!

Keep in mind that the effects of alcohol may be dramatically worsened as a result of an interaction with another drug or medicine. If a person appears to be considerably more intoxicated than is warranted by the amount of alcohol consumed, try to find out if he or she has taken any drugs. If the victim says that other drugs were consumed, try to find out what they were and when they were taken—and then contact a doctor.

If a person is so drunk that he or she is barely conscious or is unconscious, you must take certain first-aid steps until medical attention arrives.

● Place the victim in the recovery position. The victim should be on his stomach with his left leg drawn slightly up.
● Send for medical help.

Remember, never give alcohol to an injured person who may be suffering from shock. Alcohol may only enhance the shock symptoms or aggravate the problem.

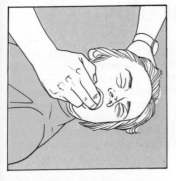

If the victim of overdrinking is in a state of collapse or seems to be choking, turn him on his back and dislodge any object (including dentures) or fluid in the mouth.

Open the airway by tilting the head back. Push the jaw forward to lift tongue. If the victim still has trouble breathing, you may have to begin artificial respiration.

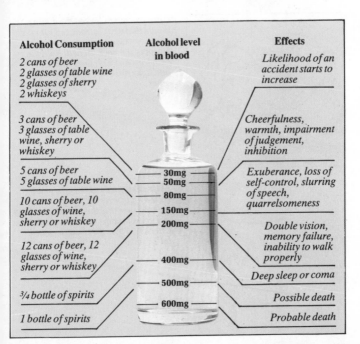

Alcohol Consumption	Alcohol level in blood	Effects
2 cans of beer 2 glasses of table wine 2 glasses of sherry 2 whiskeys		Likelihood of an accident starts to increase
3 cans of beer 3 glasses of table wine, sherry or whiskey		Cheerfulness, warmth, impairment of judgement, inhibition
5 cans of beer 5 glasses of table wine	30mg 50mg 80mg	Exuberance, loss of self-control, slurring of speech, quarrelsomeness
10 cans of beer, 10 glasses of wine, sherry or whiskey	150mg 200mg	Double vision, memory failure, inability to walk properly
12 cans of beer, 12 glasses of wine, sherry or whiskey	400mg	
	500mg	Deep sleep or coma
¾ bottle of spirits	600mg	Possible death
1 bottle of spirits		Probable death

ARTIFICIAL RESPIRATION

If a victim is unconscious or begins to have serious difficulty breathing, you must act quickly! Call for help. Loosen the victim's clothing and gently tap the victim's face. If you do not get a response, listen closely at the victim's mouth and check the abdomen and chest for any movement showing that the victim is breathing on his own. If you are certain breathing has ceased, you must administer artificial respiration. Also called mouth-to-mouth resuscitation and sometimes called ventilation, artificial respiration is a way of forcing air into the victim's lungs.

Follow these steps to give artificial respiration: ADULTS

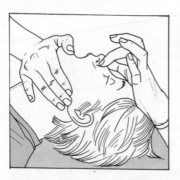

Once you have cleared the airway, it is vital that air is introduced into the casualty's lungs as soon as possible. Keeping the neck arched, hold the chin forward with one hand and pinch the nostrils closed with the other.

After taking a deep breath, place your mouth over the casualty's, making sure that the seal is tight. Give five good breaths into the mouth. Check whether the chest rises and falls.

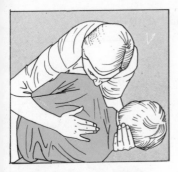

If there is no sign of breathing, *the airway may still be blocked. Pull the casualty onto his side toward you and give two sharp slaps between the shoulder blades.*

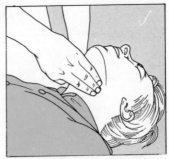

If the chest has risen, *check the pulse on the neck carefully (it may be barely perceptible) before continuing artificial respiration. If there is no sign of a pulse, begin heart massage.*

If there is a pulse *and the chest has risen, give another good breath into the casualty's mouth, checking to see whether the chest again rises.*

Once the chest has gone down, *give another good breath into the mouth. Continue in this way, giving a breath every five seconds, until the casualty starts to breathe normally. Place in the recovery position and stay with the victim until medical help arrives.*

13

BABIES AND INFANTS

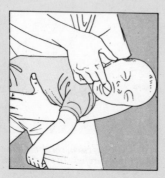

Place the baby on your knee, *supporting its trunk and head. Tilt the head back slightly and clear the mouth of any obstruction.*

Cover both the baby's nose and mouth *with your own mouth and give a gentle breath into the baby's lungs, watching for the chest to rise.*

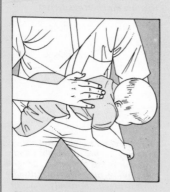

If the chest does not rise, *turn the baby over and, supporting it carefully, give a gentle tap between the shoulder blades. Resume artificial respiration.*

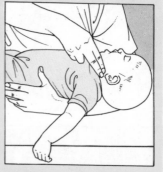

Check for a pulse on the baby's neck *(it may be very faint). If none is present, start heart massage immediately. Otherwise, continue to give one gentle breath every two seconds until the baby begins to breathe normally.*

CHILDREN

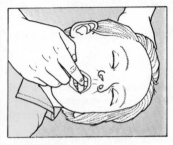

With the child's head to one side, clear the mouth of any obstruction.

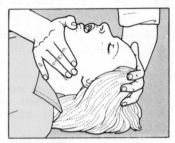

Tilt the head back and open the mouth by holding the forehead and chin.

Pinch the nostrils closed and give five good breaths into the mouth.

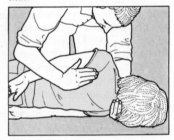

If the chest does not rise, slap the child between the shoulder blades.

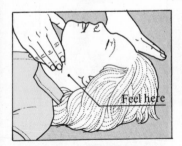

Feel for a pulse on the neck. If absent, begin heart massage. If present, give two more short breaths into the child's mouth.

Continue giving breaths once every five seconds until normal breathing resumes, when the child should be placed in the recovery position.

BACK AND NECK INJURIES

Back and neck injuries fall into two main categories: injuries of the spine and muscular strains.

FRACTURES
A violent injury to the spine may involve damage to both the spinal vertebrae and the spinal cord. Such injuries are extremely dangerous. Any victim of a road accident or serious fall may have suffered spinal damage.

If a person has suffered a back or neck injury, follow these steps:
● Do not make any attempt to move the victim if you suspect that the spine may be fractured.
● Summon medical help.
● If the victim is conscious, ask him to wiggle his toes and fingers, but prevent him from moving any other parts of his body. If the fingers and toes cannot be moved, this suggests a serious injury.
● If help is on the way, keep the head and neck still. Support the victim's head with a pillow on either side of—not underneath—the head. Do not move the victim. Keep the person calm until the medical help arrives.

Working at a desk that is too low or sitting in a hunched position are common causes of back complaints.

Make sure that your working surface is at a comfortable level and keep your spine straight when sitting.

Back and Neck Strains

Strained muscles are quite common, particularly in sports, and occur when the muscles are over-stretched. In some severe back strain cases, the muscles may actually be torn by over-exertion. If there is any doubt, treat the injury as a potential fracture.

Strained back and neck muscles should be treated by rest and, if necessary, medical help. Immediately after the injury, the application of ice to the area may help to relieve the pain. Later on, a heating pad on the affected muscles can be very soothing.

Slipped Disk

Fleshy pads (disks) between the vertebrae of the spine link the vertebrae together and act as shock absorbers when the back moves. A rupture of one of these pads is commonly called a slipped disk. Such ruptures most often occur in the lower back, usually as a result of lifting a heavy object improperly. Because the rupture puts pressure on the spinal cord, the primary symptom is usually sudden, sharp pain in one or both legs; sometimes there is numbness in the leg. In a severe case, the rupture presses against the root of a nerve and can cause pain that goes the length of the leg, from the upper thigh to the sole of the foot. This pain is sometimes referred to as sciatica.

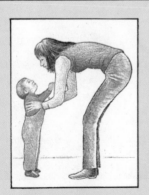

Lifting even a very young child can cause back injury if done incorrectly. Lift from a crouching position by bending the knees and then straightening up, rather than bending down from the waist.

BANDAGES AND DRESSINGS

Bandages and dressings are protective coverings that are normally applied directly to wounds to help control bleeding, absorb any discharge, and lessen the risk of infection.

Bandages are used to keep dressings in place. In addition, they are used to provide support and prevent movement in the case of a fracture, giving the damaged bones an opportunity to heal.

It is not difficult, in theory, to tie a bandage or apply a dressing. However, the stress of coping with an emergency often makes it more difficult. The first priority is always to stop serious bleeding.

Whenever possible, wash your hands before dressing a wound. This helps to prevent infection. Once the bleeding is under control, clean the wound before bandaging it. Always apply a dressing directly on the wound; never slide it into position.

Keep a variety of bandages and dressings in a first-aid kit. In an emergency, however, use anything that comes to hand as a bandage, as long as it is clean. Never use fluffy dressings over open

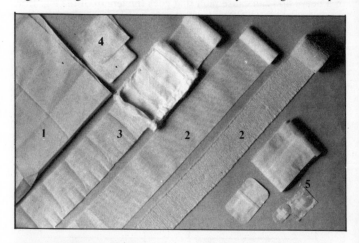

Of the different types available, a triangular bandage (1) is the most adaptable to different needs. A roller bandage (2) is used to keep a dressing in place. Large wounds should be protected by sterile, unmedicated dressings (3). Gauze dressings (4) provide a light covering for burns. Use adhesive dressings (5) for minor wounds.

wounds, as they will stick to the injury and make changing the dressing a painful experience.

There are many different types of bandages available, each suited to a specific purpose. Some you can make yourself. One of the most useful bandages is the triangular bandage. What makes this bandage unique is its adaptability. By folding the bandage at various widths, the triangular bandage becomes the universal item in your first-aid kit. A triangular bandage for use as a sling can be cut from a linen or cloth square. Once made, the bandage can be converted into a broad or narrow one simply by folding it. Fold the point of the triangle toward its base, having first created a narrow hem along it. Then, fold the bandage in half and, to narrow it still further, fold in half once more.

Sterile, unmedicated adhesive dressings are recommended by doctors as the best possible protection for large wounds. They are available in a variety of shapes and sizes to suit various injuries. The dressings consist of a cotton pad and layers of soft gauze, mounted on a bandage. They are factory-sealed in protective wrappings.

HOW TO FOLD A TRIANGULAR BANDAGE

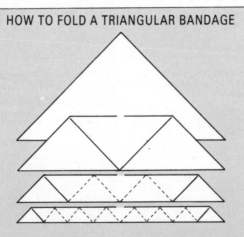

A triangle cut from a square piece of clean linen serves as a sling or an all-purpose bandage. To make a bandage, fold the top point to the middle of the base, which should have a narrow, folded hem. Continue folding depending on the broadness of bandage you require.

MAKING A RING BANDAGE

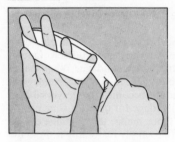

Wind a narrow bandage around fingers to make a loop.

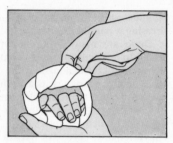

Pass the other end of the bandage through the loop. Wind it around the loop and pull tight.

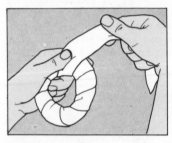

Continue winding until you have a solid ring and the bandage is used up. Tuck in the end.

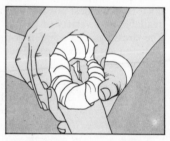

Put the end of a securing bandage under the ring before placing it over the injury.

Wrap the bandage over the limb and over the ring twice then, working diagonally, continue until the ring is properly secure.

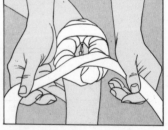

Any suitable, clean material — a tie for example, or a scarf — can be used in an emergency to construct a ring bandage.

USING A ROLLER BANDAGE

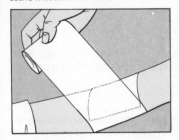

Place one end of the bandage around the injury.

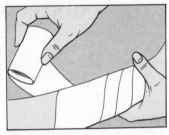

Wrap it around the wound once, then work up the limb in a series of spirals. Secure the end.

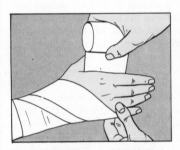

Bandage hand in manner shown, up to the nail of the little finger.

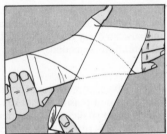

Cross-cross the palm and the back of the hand. Cut the remaining bandage into two ribbons and knot in place.

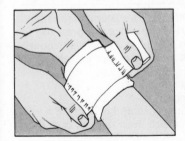

After washing your hands, center the dressing over the wound, with the gauze side down.

Wind the bandage around the limb to secure the dressing. Finish with a square knot, making sure that the circulation is not constricted.

21

BITES AND STINGS

Bites and stings, whether from insects or animals, are rarely dangerous, although they may cause pain and discomfort and frequently cause shock in the victim.

ANIMAL BITES
Animal bites that are not very deep and involve no puncture marks should be treated like a simple cut (see "Cuts, Scratches, and Abrasions"). However, if the bite comes from a human or if it is very deep or has puncture marks, a doctor should be seen. A tetanus shot may be needed.

If it is at all possible, the biting animal should be caught and checked for rabies. (This does not harm the animal.) Dogs are not the only animals to carry rabies—cats, foxes, racoons and other animals can carry it as well. If rabies is suspected, immediate medical attention is needed.

SNAKE BITES
Rattlesnakes, copperheads, cottonmouths and coral snakes are the most common poisonous snakes in the United States. A bite from any of these snakes requires immediate action.

If the bite is from a coral snake, keep the victim still and summon medical help. If the bite is from a rattlesnake, copperhead, or cottonmouth, follow the steps in the table below:

RATTLESNAKE, COPPERHEAD OR COTTONMOUTH BITES

- Kill the snake if possible and save it for later identification.
- Wrap a band around the bitten arm or leg at a point two to four inches above the bite. Do not pull the band tight enough to cut off the circulation. A belt or piece of rope makes a good band.
- Wash the bite area with soap and water.
- Do not apply ice to the area.
- With a sterile razor blade or very sharp knife, make a vertical incision about one-quarter inch deep through each fang mark. Do not make an X through the marks.
- Using a sucking cup or the mouth, suck out the venom. Spit out the venom.
- Get medical help.

Brown recluse spider

Black widow spider with the hourglass on its underside

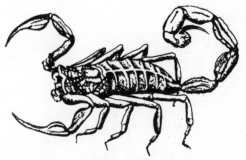

Scorpion

INSECT BITES OR STINGS

Insect bites and stings are most commonly caused by bees, wasps, ants, scorpions and spiders. Some people suffer an allergic reaction to certain bites, and if this is severe, the victim may require resuscitation and immediate hospitalization.

● Venomous spider bites should be treated as for snake bites.

● Other insect stings or bites should be treated with cold compresses or with an ice pack if available.

● If still present in the wound, stings should be carefully removed. Bites or stings to the head or neck, especially the mouth area, require hospital treatment.

● Keep the victim under observation for any signs of allergic reaction. Should the casualty lose consciousness, commence airway breathing and respiratory treatment immediately and take to hospital as soon as possible.

BLEEDING

Wounds are divided into two categories: open, when blood escapes from the body, and closed, when blood escapes internally into body cavities from the circulatory system. In the case of internal bleeding the only visible sign of bleeding may be bruises under the skin in some instances.

In all cases, the priority is to stop the bleeding as soon as possible. Continuous blood loss can lead to death. The body will be taking its own steps to help you in your task, as the blood-clotting factors work to clot the blood, while the blood pressure drops to restrict the blood flow.

Open Wounds

In the first instance, *try to stanch bleeding from a large wound by squeezing the sides of the injury firmly with your fingers (above). If possible, lay the casualty down and keep the injured limb raised while continuing to maintain pressure (right). In the case of a small cut, simply placing your hand over the wound and applying steady pressure (above, right) may be sufficient to stem the flow of blood.*

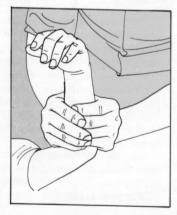

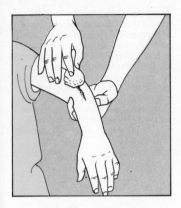

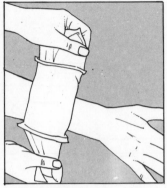

When treating a cut, *laceration, or similar injury, it is important to limit the chances of infection by removing any dirt. After bleeding has stopped, clean the edges of the wound with swabs soaked in warm water. Use a fresh swab as each one becomes soiled, taking care not to dislodge the blood clot that will have formed.*

Pressing down firmly, *apply a sterile, unmedicated dressing that is large enough to extend well beyond the wound. Secure the dressing with a bandage. Gauze and absorbent cotton can also be used as a dressing. Remember to position the gauze before the cotton, which if placed directly on the wound may disturb the clot on removal.*

PRESSURE POINTS

If a wound is bleeding so badly that direct pressure on it doesn't help, or if the wound is so large that direct pressure can't be applied, you can apply direct pressure to the artery between the injured area and the heart. Press the artery hard at a point where it is near a bone. For the arms, apply the pressure to the brachial artery, the artery that runs along the inside of the upper arm; for a wound on the hand, press the artery on the victim's wrist. For the legs, apply the pressure to the femoral artery, the artery that runs down the inner thigh. Pressure points on the head are found on either side of the neck both just below and just above the ears.

25

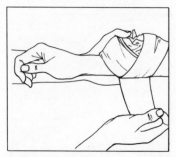

A puncture wound may be more serious than it looks because the point of entry may be quite small in relation to the depth of the injury. If the blood flow is not too profuse, do not attempt to stop it, but allow the blood to carry out any dirt that may have penetrated the wound. Once the bleeding has stopped and a clot has formed, wash the wound and cover it with a sterile dressing. An anti-tetanus injection may be necessary, so take the casualty to a doctor.

INTERNAL BLEEDING

A victim with no visible external injuries could still be bleeding internally. The symptoms of internal bleeding are very similar to those for shock: the victim is pale and sweaty, has a weak pulse, and may have trouble breathing. He may feel cold and very thirsty. In addition, he may cough up or vomit blood; there may be blood in the urine.

If you suspect internal bleeding, summon medical help at once. Treat the victim for shock (see "Shock").

TOURNIQUETS

If you feel that you have to resort to the use of a tourniquet (a band tied tightly above the injury) to stem very heavy bleeding, remember that it can be dangerous. A tourniquet should be applied only in life-threatening situations where bleeding cannot be controlled by any other method. If direct pressure on the wound or to a pressure point does not stop the flow of blood, then a tourniquet may be considered.

The decision to use a tourniquet means you must choose between saving the victim's life and risking the injured limb. Using a tourniquet can lead to losing the limb, since the circulation is cut off. However, a tourniquet can save a life if used properly.

In all tourniquet cases, medical assistance should be summoned at once. In general, the nature of the injury will be so severe that you'd probably be calling for medical attention anyway.

Once you've made the decision to apply a tourniquet, it is vital that you do it correctly:

● The tourniquet is placed just above the wound. Although it shouldn't touch the bleeding area directly, the closer you get it to the injured area the more effective it will be. If the serious wound is near a joint such as a knee or elbow, place the tourniquet above the joint.

● Most people do not keep a tourniquet handy. Use anything! Rip off a piece of clothing, for example, and wrap it around the limb at least twice. Then tie it in a knot, leaving long ends.

● Find a small, hard, straight object—in a pinch you can use a stick, pencil, or even a fork. Place it over the tourniquet's knot.

● Use the ends of the knot and tie another knot to secure the stick to the tourniquet.

● Grab the stick and begin twisting it to tighten the tourniquet around the limb. Keep tightening until the bleeding stops.

● Use another piece of cloth and tie the stick in place a little further up the limb away from the wound.

In certain circumstances where the bleeding is severe and unstoppable but not enough to pose an immediate threat to life, you could use a modified tourniquet method. Apply the tourniquet as above and tighten it to stop the flow of blood. Then count to 15 and loosen the tourniquet. This allows the circulation to return to the limb, preventing permanent damage. If bleeding continues, repeat the process. This should give the body's natural clotting mechanism a chance to react to the wound.

Remember, the use of the tourniquet is itself dangerous. Summon medical help as you begin the procedure.

BONE INJURIES

In an injury, bones may fracture, or become dislocated at the point where they meet in a joint. Of these conditions, a fracture is potentially the most serious, so if there's any doubt, treat the injury as if it were a fracture.

The most serious kind of fracture is when the damaged bone has broken through the skin. This is called a compound or open fracture and the risk of subsequent infection is high.

A joint is dislocated when one or more of the bones meeting at the joint are displaced. There are two possible causes. A strong force can wrench the bone out of its normal position, or a sudden muscular contraction may pull the bone out of joint.

Keep in mind that the victim should not be moved at all. Break this rule only if there is a risk of further injury should the victim remain in the same place.

The general first aid that can be applied to the victims of all bone injuries involves immobilizing or supporting the affected limbs for movement to medical help.

SPLINTS

A splint is used to immobilize an injured limb. In an emergency, a splint must usually be improvised. Anything that is fairly rigid and flat can be used—a broomstick, a branch, even a rolled-up newspaper or magazine. Place the splint alongside the injured limb. To attach it you may have to improvise some more. Use an elastic bandage, rope, a belt or strap, or strips of cloth to bind it firmly but gently to the victim at several points. Never force the limb to move and don't bind the splint on tightly enough to affect the circulation.

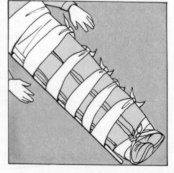

Limit movement by using a splint for an injured leg or tying both legs together for an injured pelvis.

ARMS

For lower arm injuries, often involving the wrist or forearm, a sling can be used to immobilize the area. Here are the simple steps:

Place the injured limb *across the casualty's chest. Use padding if the wrist or forearm is involved.*

Fit a triangular bandage *so that one end lies over the shoulder of the uninjured arm.*

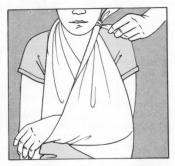

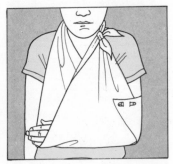

Take the bandage *around the back of the neck to the front of the body on the injured side. Supporting the limb all the while, carry the bandage up over the affected area and tie above the collar bone with a square knot (above, left). Secure the loose point at the elbow by using a safety pin to attach it to the front of the bandage (above). For additional support, wrap a broad bandage over the sling and around the chest (left).*

29

AN ELEVATION SLING

An elevation sling is needed for chest and shoulder injuries. Position the appropriate forearm diagonally across the casualty's chest. Ease the base of a triangular bandage under the arm and carry one end over the back to meet the other at the front of the uninjured shoulder. Tie the ends with a square knot above the collar bone and secure the loose point.

If the elbow is damaged and the arm is extended, do not ask the casualty to bend his or her arm as you would when making a normal sling — you may cause further injury. Instead, place the arm alongside the casualty's body and use several broad bandages to keep it in position. If possible, attach a splint to the arm before transporting the casualty (which should be attempted only by stretcher).

When giving first aid for an injured arm, keep in mind that all you're doing is making it safer for the victim to be transported. The more the injured arm is jostled, the greater the chance of further injury. Using a splint and a sling with a broad body bandage prevents any unnecessary movement of the damaged bone. Check the victim to see if there are any signs of shock; if so, treat it (see "Shock"). Do not offer the victim anything to eat or drink because this could be dangerous if medical treatment of the injury necessitates a general anesthetic.

LEGS

Leg bone injuries usually involve the bones of the lower leg: the tibia or the fibula. Tibia fractures are often compound because the bone is covered by only a thin layer of skin and tissue. Fibula fractures often occur as the result of an ankle wrench and can easily be mistaken at first for a severely strained ankle.

When a leg bone is damaged you should:

Support the injured limb and gently move it alongside the undamaged one. Place padding between the knees and ankles and bandage the legs together, using a figure-of-eight bandage for the ankles and a broad bandage for the knees. If it seems necessary, increase the number of bandages, wrapping one around the thighs, one around the lower legs and one below the injury. Do not place a bandage directly around the injured site, because pressure on the area could cause further damage. If there is a suitable splint in the vicinity (it should reach from the upper thigh down to the foot) place it alongside the injured leg before putting the padding and bandages in position. Unless the leg swells around the ankle, it is best not to remove the casualty's shoe because it provides valuable extra support for the injured limb.

Injuries to the femur (thigh bone) should be treated like other leg injuries, except that they require added support. A long splint, running from armpit to foot, should be bound along the outer side of the injured thigh. Place a second splint alongside the inner thigh of the injured leg. Secure the splints individually and then use broad bandages, wrapping around the leg, pelvis, and chest, to keep everything in place.

If a victim appears to have injured a hip or the pelvis, do not try to move him to prevent damage to internal organs or the spine.

ANKLE AND FOOT INJURIES

With an ankle or foot injury, do not remove the footwear unless serious swelling occurs. The shoe or sneaker gives support to the injured area. Keep weight off the damaged limb and support the foot from the knee down with cushions and pillows.

Kneecap fractures occur when the small bone in the front of the knee breaks as a result of a blow or muscle strain. Knees can also be dislocated.

Limit movement by using a splint for an injured leg or tying both legs together for an injured pelvis.

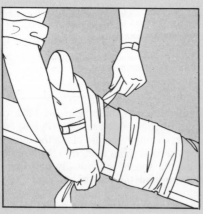

Place the injured limb across the casualty's chest. Use padding if the wrist or forearm is involved.

BURNS

Burns can be among the most serious of common accidents. They carry an associated risk of shock and infection, and can leave bad scars. The dangers for babies and children are especially serious because of the proportionally larger area of skin affected by even a minor burn and the increased chance and severity of shock.

In most cases other than minor first-degree burns, medical attention is necessary. If burning is extensive, send for an ambulance immediately.

Burns may be caused by the sun, by flame or heat, chemicals, electricity (see "Electric Shock"), or friction. Scalds are caused by hot liquids, such as cooking oil or steam. The effects are much the same.

BASIC FIRST-AID STEPS FOR BURNS

● Cool the area of the burn by placing it under cold running water. If the burn area is too large to hold under a faucet, then immerse it in cold water. If this is not possible because of the nature and location of the burn, then pour cold water over the area. Apply cold water for at least 10 minutes. However, do not apply ice to a burn. If the burn is large or deep, get medical help immediately.

● If the skin has been scalded and the clothing over the scald is still warm, then remove it. The heat retained by the clothing may do further damage.

● If the clothing has been burnt, do not remove it. It will stick to the burn and should be removed only by trained medical personnel.

● If the burn has been caused by chemicals, remove any clothing that may have been soaked with the chemicals. Remember to protect your own hands before handling the clothing.

● If the burn is not serious, apply a sterile dressing. *Do not* use an adhesive dressing, which may stick to the affected area. *Do not* use cotton balls, for the same reason. *Do not* apply any ointment or grease to the burn. It does not help and will just have to be painfully cleaned off later. Do not puncture any blisters.

● If the burn is very severe, try to use a calming tone when addressing the victim. Your reassuring voice may prevent a panic situation.

CHOKING

The most common cause of choking is a physical obstruction to breathing. Most often this is caused by a particle of food or gulp of liquid that "has gone done the wrong pipe". In other words, the piece of food has been taken into the airway instead of the esophagus (the tube that leads to the stomach).

People often "swallow wrong" and choke momentarily. In most cases, the object is coughed up easily. If someone is coughing hard but has a normal complexion or is red in the face from the coughing, leave him alone—he will probably be all right without help. However, if someone has a bluish colour, and is coughing weakly or not at all, cannot speak or breathe, and clutches at his throat, he is in serious trouble and you must act immediately.

First, put your finger deep into the mouth of the victim and try to remove anything that may be blocking the upper airway—but be careful not to push it deeper instead.

If that doesn't help, follow these steps:

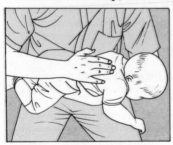

If the victim of choking is a baby, support the chest and abdomen and smack gently between the shoulder blades.

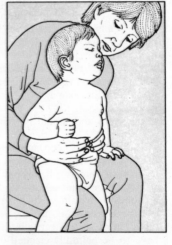

If this does not dislodge the obstruction, place two fingertips together just above the baby's navel and press gently upward.

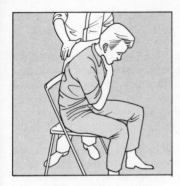

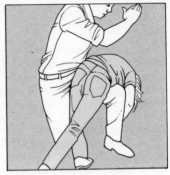

If the victim is sitting (left), hit him sharply between the shoulder blades with the heel of your hand. Preferably, bend the victim's body

so that the head is lower than the chest (right). Grasp a choking child (below) around the stomach and give a sharp squeeze.

● If the victim has fallen down, turn him on his side toward you, with his chest pressing against your thighs for support. Then reach over and give him four sharp hits between the shoulder blades, as in the first step above.
● If after trying the above methods, the person is still choking, it's time to apply the Heimlich maneuver. Stand behind the victim. Make a fist, reach around and press the fist, thumb first, into the victim's abdomen just below the ribcage. Cover the fist with your other hand. Pull the fist sharply in and upward into the victim's abdomen, much as if you were hugging the victim. This maneuver forces a rush of air up through the airway, which will probably dislodge the obstruction.

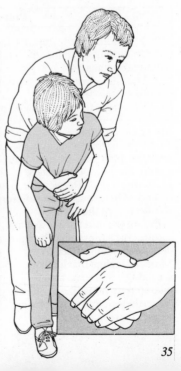

CONVULSIONS

Convulsions are uncontrollable fits of muscle spasm, in which the limbs twitch, the eyes roll and there may be resultant loss of consciousness. In infants and small children they are usually associated with a high fever. In adults, epilepsy is the usual cause, although convulsions may be seen after a drug overdose.

CHILDHOOD CONVULSIONS

Convulsions in babies and small children are generally short and not serious. However, any convulsion lasting for more than two or three minutes or in which breathing stops should be considered a medical emergency. Send for medical help immediately. The symptoms are twitching limbs, rolling eyes, a red, congested face, frothy saliva and an arched back with the breath held. Childhood convulsions are most often caused by a high fever.

CHILDREN

- Do not attempt to restrain the child.
- Do not put anything into the child's mouth to keep it from biting the tongue.
- After the seizure has passed, place the child in the recovery position (see "Recovery").
- Take steps to reduce the fever.

ADULT CONVULSIONS

Adults with epilepsy may suffer from either of the two forms of seizures: petit mal or grand mal. The symptoms of a petit mal seizure are lack of awareness of surroundings, paleness, and fixed or staring eyes. The seizure is usually brief, often lasting only seconds. On recovery, the sufferer has no recollection of the event.

Before the onset of a grand mal seizure, the sufferer may be warned of the impending attack by an "aura, or feeling that a seizure is coming", and so be able to take steps to minimize its effects. Nevertheless, during a grand mal seizure there may be loss of consciousness, with rigidity and

ADULTS

● Do not try to restrain the victim.
● Do not attempt to put anything into the mouth to keep him from biting his tongue.
● The seizure will generally pass quickly, leaving the victim somewhat dazed. However, a seizure that lasts more than two to three minutes or in which the breathing stops is a medical emergency—send for help.
● Check to see if the victim has any obstructions, such as dentures or vomit in the throat after the seizure.
● Adult seizure victims commonly pass through a stage of embarrassment following a seizure. A calm, reassuring voice is needed here.
● If a victim warns you that an attack is coming on, place him on the floor. During the attack, try to turn the victim's head to the side to prevent any choking should he vomit. If this proves difficult, try to turn the victim over on the stomach.

RECOVERY POSITION

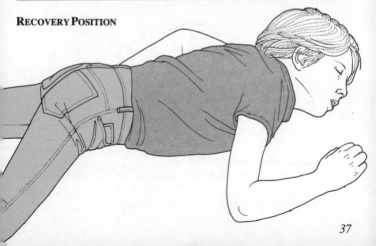

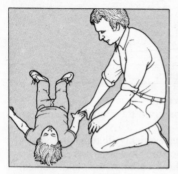

Putting a child into the recovery position: 1 *Loosen clothing.*

2 *Place nearest arm under the buttocks. Place other arm on chest.*

3 *Cross the leg farthest away from you over the other leg.*

4 *Roll the child toward you and support him against your knees.*

5 *Bend top leg at knee. Place top arm beside head. Pull other arm out.*

6 *Carefully lift the head up and back to aid breathing.*

CUTS, SCRAPES, ABRASIONS AND BLISTERS

Minor cuts, scratches, and abrasions (scrapes) rarely need major medical attention. However, if they are not treated properly, infection can set in.

For most cuts and scratches, the body's response is the eventual formation of a scab over the wound to ward off germs and protect it as it heals. First aid in the form of an antiseptic rinse and cleansing should be performed before the scab forms.

There are six simple steps to treating cuts and scratches:

CUTS AND SCRATCHES

 Wash your hands with warm, soapy water. The only safe way to treat the victim's wound is with clean hands.

 Using a gauze pad or sterile cotton balls, cleanse the minor wound. The easiest way to do this is by dipping the gauze or cotton in a solution of mild disinfectant and water. The trick here is to bathe the wound by working the gauze in a motion through or away from the cut. This way you gently sweep out any foreign particles, leaving the wound free for the formation of the scab.

 Using a fresh gauze pad or cotton balls, gently dab the wound dry. The body secretes its own moisture and an overabundance of fluids might lead to infection.

 Dress the wound. Depending on the size and nature of the cut, select a gauze pad and cover the injured area with it. Tape the pad in place. Of course, if the cut is small enough a simple adhesive bandage would be sufficient.

 Despite all the advertising, it's not necessary to apply any antiseptic cream or ointment if you've cleaned the wound properly. These lotions sometimes can actually seal in dirt and germs, increasing the likelihood of infection.

 If you notice that the cut or scratch is oozing, is very red, shows signs of inflammation, or feels tender you should consult a doctor. These are all signs of infection.

PUNCTURE WOUNDS

A deep puncture wound caused by stepping on a nail, for example, is slightly more serious than a minor cut. Because the wound is deep and usually bleeds very little, it is more likely to become infected. It is also more likely that a puncture wound can damage a tendon or nerve. Treat the wound by washing it with soap and water and applying an antiseptic. See your doctor immediately if you have not had a tetanus shot within the past ten years.

If an object is deeply embedded, prepare to make a protective ring bandage by winding a clean narrow bandage round your fingers.

Pass the loose end of the bandage round the loop until you have used the whole bandage and pull it tight.

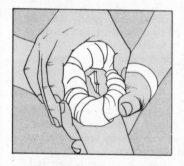

Place the ring bandage in position round the wound and attach it with a second bandage taken under the ring first.

Work the second securing bandage around the ring diagonally, under the limb and over the ring until it is absolutely secure.

BLISTERS
A blister is a fluid-filled bubble that develops between two layers of the skin. It may be caused by a burn, sunburn, or by friction—from badly fitting shoes or boots, particularly ones that are loose at the heel, for example. Although a blister is a result of damage to the skin, it also has an important part to play in the healing process. A blister forms to protect the underlying tissue and allow regeneration to take place.

If the blister is not broken, never try to prick it open or tear it off. Allow the blister to come off naturally. To protect the blister until this occurs, cut a hole in a gauze pad and place over the blister. Then tape the pad loosely in place, allowing the blister to breathe. In due course, the blister will dry out and the skin on top will come off.

If the blister is in an area where it is likely to break, such as on the foot or hand, you may want to drain it, although the damaged area may hurt more after draining.

To drain a blister you should:
● Clean the blister area with soap and water.
● Sterilize a needle over a match or candle flame to sterilize it. Let the needle cool, but do not touch the tip with anything, as this will only deposit germs.
● Prick an edge of the blister with the point of the needle.
● Using a sterile gauze pad, gently press the blister to drain the fluid, moving slowing from one side to the other.
● After the blister has been drained, cover it with a clean gauze pad or adhesive bandage.

If the blister is already torn and draining, you should still take the precaution of dressing the wound. Again, clean the area with soap and water. Then press out any remaining fluid with a sterile gauze pad. Take another sterile pad and tape it into place over the blistered area. Alternatively use special blister plasters, obtainable from most pharmacies.

Like any damaged area of the body, blisters may get infected. Watch out for any indications that infection has occurred, such as throbbing, redness, oozing, fever, or swollen glands. If you think that the blister has become infected apply an antiseptic; if that fails, consult a doctor.

DROWNING

Anyone who is in difficulty in the water—even shallow water—may be drowning or about to drown. If you know that the water is shallow and safe, wade out to the victim. Remember that a muscle cramp may prevent the victim from standing, even in shallow water. If the water is deep and you are a good swimmer and have passed a life-saving course, attempt a rescue if you feel confident of success. If the water is deep and you are untrained in life-saving, you can still aid the victim by calling for help, noting the position and by throwing the victim a rope or a float of some sort. Keep in mind that the majority of drownings occur within reach of some safety.

A swimming rescue should not be attempted unless you have taken and passed a specialized life-saving course offered by an organization such as the Red Cross. Even though you may be an excellent swimmer, you must remember that a drowning victim is in a state of panic. A drowning person will grab at anything that comes his way, including a potential rescuer.

If the victim is having trouble in shallow water, you can wade out to the location and offer assistance. Keep in mind that the trouble is probably caused by a muscle cramp and assure the victim that you are in control. Grab the victim under the armpits and pull him up to get the head out of the water. Keep talking to the victim as you move toward the shore. As soon as the victim feels safe, the fear of drowning will subside and the rescue will become easier.

If the victim is in deep water and you are untrained in life-saving, you may still try a rescue. If the victim is near the edge of a pool or the shore, lie on your stomach and extend your arm or leg; for a

A casualty of drowning who is experiencing breathing difficulties from having swallowed a large amount of water or who has stopped breathing altogether needs artificial respiration at once. If there is too much water in the lungs for resuscitation to be effective, turn the victim on his or her back and press down firmly on the back to force the water out before beginning again.

victim further out, try extending a stick or pole. Remember that a drowning person will cling to anything. Make sure that you hold on to something on shore, or you could be dragged in too!

If the victim is out of reach, look for something to throw out to the deep water. Improvise . . . use anything handy such as an oar or even a folding wooden chair.

After the victim is on the shore you should begin artificial respiration if the victim is not breathing (see "Artificial Respiration"). At the same time, get somebody to call for medical help.

If you are having trouble with the artificial respiration, there may be too much water in the lungs. Turn the victim on his stomach and press down on the back to force the water out. Then start the artificial respiration again.

In all events, a drowning victim should go to the hospital. One of the side effects of drowning is possible pneumonia from the water in the lungs.

Learn the correct distress signals so that other people know you're in trouble — they could save your life.

ELECTRIC SHOCK

Electric shock can cause unconsciousness and loss of breathing; the heart may stop. In addition, there may be a burn where the electricity entered the body, and there may be internal damage. Your job as a rescuer is to get the victim safely away from the current and to revive him if necessary.

Your first priority when going to the aid of a victim of electric shock from a domestic supply is to either turn off the current or remove the victim from the source. If it proves impossible to disconnect the current, use something that is a nonconductor of electricity to push the victim away, such as anything made of rubber, cloth or dry wood. Avoid using objects that are wet or evenly slightly damp — water is an excellent conductor of electricity.

If you can see that the current is still on—for example, if the piece of machinery is still plugged in—then try to shut it off and unplug it as soon as possible. The longer a current flows into the body, the stronger the possibility of cardiac arrest.

If you think it's impossible to disconnect the current you must try to separate the victim from the source. Push the victim away from the source with something that is a nonconductor of electricity. Useful nonconductors are dry and made of rubber, cloth, or wood. Do not use anything that is wet because water is an excellent conductor of electricity. A rolled-up newspaper or even the victim's own clothing, if dry, will prevent the transmission of the current to your own body.

Try to shut off or remove the victim from the electrical current only if the source is ordinary domestic electricity. If the victim is in contact with a high-voltage supply of electricity—a power line, for example—do not attempt a rescue. Summon medical help immediately and call the police.

After any emergency rescue from electric shock, you should call for medical help. Begin artificial respiration if the victim is not breathing (see "Artificial Respiration"). If there is no pulse and if you are qualified, begin heart massage (see "Heart Massage").

EYE INJURIES

The eye is an extremely sensitive instrument, so all eye injuries are potentially serious.

The commonest cause of injury is a foreign body in the eye. Dust, grit, and loose eyelashes can all adhere to the surface of the eyeball or get caught under the eyelid. In addition, flying fragments of glass, metal, and grit can cut or bruise the surface of the eye and can cause serious injury if not removed.

If there is a foreign body in the eye that blinking does not quickly remove, ask the victim not to rub it. Sit the victim in a chair facing a light and tilt the head back. Separate the eyelids and examine the eye carefully. When you locate the foreign object, wash the eye out with clean water or use a moistened cotton swab to gently remove it. If nothing else is available, use the moistened corner of a handkerchief or tissue. If the foreign object appears to be imbedded, seek medical help.

If the foreign object is trapped under the upper lid, ask the victim to look down, rather than up. Take hold of the eyelashes and pull the upper eyelid downward and outward, so that the lashes can brush the object away. If this fails try blinking the eye under water to float the object off.

Another hint to keep in mind is that in today's world many people wear contact lenses. If someone is having trouble with an eye, make sure to ask if it might be a problem with contacts.

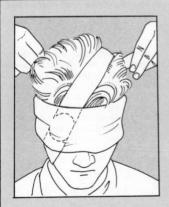

Protect an injured eye with a sterile pad, secured by a bandage. The pad will not only soak up any blood or fluid that leaks from the wound, but also provide protection against infection. If the injury seems serious, wrap a bandage around both eyes to keep the sound eye from moving: any movement of one eye causes the other to move too, which may worsen the injury. Medical help should be sought immediately.

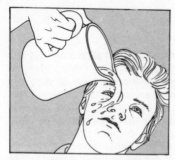

Any chemical that has accidentally entered the eye should immediately be flushed out with clean, cold water for at least 15 minutes. It may be necessary for the casualty to hold the affected eye open or to place his or her head under water and blink continuously. Do not apply ointment, but secure a pad over the eye with a bandage and call for medical help.

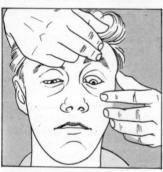

If there is a foreign body in the eye ask the casualty to face the light and tilt the head back. Carefully separate the eyelids.

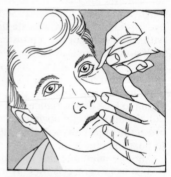

Wash the eye out with water or, if that proves ineffective, use a moistened swab or the corner of a handkerchief to remove the object.

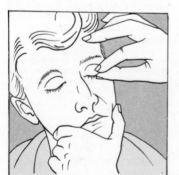

A foreign body trapped under the upper lid calls for different treatment. After asking the casualty to look down, take hold of the upper lashes and pull the eyelid downward and upward so that the lashes are able to brush the object out. If this does not work, blinking the eye under water may float the object away. If none of the methods outlined above is successful, seek medical help.

FAINTING

Simply put, a faint is a sudden, usually short, period of unconsciousness. It is a result of a temporarily reduced supply of blood to the brain. Since most fainting-related injuries occur as the victim falls, it is recommended that a person who feels faint sit down. Some of the reasons for fainting are shock, fright, exhaustion, and sudden movements after a long period of standing still. Often the victim feels suddenly dizzy and weak before fainting. The victim may also start to sweat and become pale in the face. If caught at this stage, fainting may be avoided if the person sits in a chair with the head lowered between the knees to bring more blood to the head.

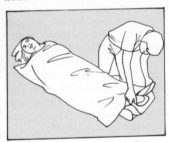

A person who has fainted should be laid gently on the ground with a support, such as a pillow or a rolled up article of clothing, placed under the legs to keep them raised. Loosen any restrictive clothing, and make sure that the casualty is warm and has a plentiful supply of air.

The last thing the victim wants is to regain consciousness while surrounded by a group of inquisitive strangers. Try to keep other people away.

If the victim begins to vomit, roll him onto his side so that the substances can't block the throat, causing choking.

If the person is having trouble regaining consciousness, you may try wafting some ammonia or smelling salts under the nose.

When the victim regains consciousness, reassure him that everything is all right. Give the victim small sips of cold water only if you're convinced that he is completely revived. After a while it's permissible to let the person have a hot, sweet drink. Under no circumstances should you give alcohol.

Determine if the victim's fall has caused any injuries.

If a fainting victim doesn't regain consciousness quickly, call for medical help. Be prepared to administer artificial respiration (see "Artificial Respiration") if necessary.

A person who frequently faints may have a more serious underlying problem. Consult a physician.

FINGERS AND TOES

Damage to a finger or toe—for example, a finger trapped in a car door or something heavy dropped on the toe—can cause agonizing pain. Besides the potential for fractures, blows to the toes and fingers may lead to bleeding under the nail, swelling, and the eventual loss of the nail.

If a finger or toe is damaged, put the injured part under the cold-water tap. Cold water will immediately help to reduce the swelling and pain. After the initial period, place an ice pack on the finger or toe for about 20 minutes.

If the finger or toe is badly bruised under or around the nail, it will be quite painful, especially if there is a lot of swelling under the nail. If the swelling is very severe, a doctor may have to puncture the nail to release the pressure. It is also possible that the nail will eventually fall off as part of the natural healing process. In the meantime, you can protect the damaged nail with a gauze pad held in place with adhesive tape.

After most finger or toe injuries the victim feels a throbbing sensation in the digit. Assure the person that the throbbing is just the body sending blood carrying natural antibodies to the injury. The human body's defense mechanism triggers a circulatory response to damaged areas. This increased circulation causes the throbbing sensation.

SEVERED DIGITS

A finger or toe that has been accidentally cut off could be rejoined to the body if you take prompt action. Take emergency measure to control the bleeding (see "Bleeding"). The severed part must be kept clean and cold. If possible, put into a plastic bag; then place the bag into another plastic bag filled with ice. Do not, however, place the severed part into water. If no ice is available, simply put the part in a clean container. Get the victim and the severed part to an emergency room as quickly as possible. Be sure to tell the emergency personnel that you have the severed part.

INGROWN TOENAIL

An ingrown toenail can be very painful. It happens when the sides of the toenail begin to curve into the flesh instead of growing out normally. Besides the pain associated with the ingrown condition, the damaged toe may get infected.

If you have an ingrown toenail, try to catch it early. Put a piece of cotton under the ingrown nail to try to force the nail back to its normal growth. Change the cotton every day. If this doesn't help wrap some cotton pads around the toe and nail to prevent any movement on the sensitive area. If the nail is very ingrown, you'll have to see a doctor or podiatrist (foot specialist).

If you have a tendency toward ingrown tailnails, try to prevent them by cutting the nails short, leaving the sides longer than the middle.

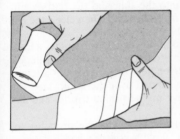

To bandage hands or feet following injury to digits, begin by winding the bandage round the limb some distance away from the point of injury.

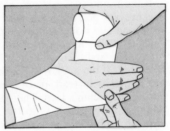

Bring the bandage across the wrist in a diagonal and wind one loop round the hand between the thumb and the forefinger.

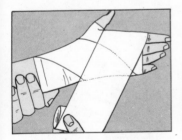

Wind the bandage over the back of the hand and round again right up to the root of the nail of the little finger. Bring the bandage back to the wrist.

To secure the bandage at the wrist, cut down the center of the bandage to form two narrow ribbons and tie these off at the bottom with a reef knot.

FISHHOOKS

A fishhook in the skin can best be removed by a doctor. However, since most fishhook related injuries take place in the country, far from any medical services, it's a good idea to be prepared to deal with it yourself. The only tools you'll need are a pair of pliers (commonly found in any bait and tackle box) and some sterile gauze pads (which should be in a small first-aid kit).

If the fishhook is just poking into the skin and the barb is still sticking out, pull the hook away from the skin. Then clean the cut with soap and water and apply the gauze dressing.

If the hook is imbedded in the skin, the situation becomes a little tricky. The first thing you must do is determine where the fishhook is located. If the hook is in the region near the eye, do not attempt to remove it. Instead, place a gauze pad over the hook; tape the pad to the victim's face. Then give up the fishing trip for the day and take the victim to a doctor.

If the fishhook is imbedded into a finger, you can probably remove it yourself. Remember how in old Westerns a cowboy sometimes gets plucked with an arrow while sitting home on the range? No problem for Tex—he would just push that arrow through the skin, cover the wound with a piece of shirt, and ride on out of there. Essentially you're going to do the same thing!

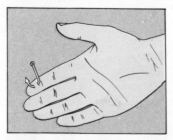

To remove a fishhook imbedded in a finger, hold the victim's hand and gently push the hook through the skin so that the pointed barb sticks out. If you have trouble, sterilize a small knife over a flame, allow it to cool, and make a tiny incision where the barb is trying to come through.

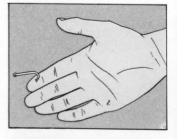

Cut the barb off with pliers and pull the hook back and out of the point of entry. Apply a dressing after having cleaned the wound. A tetanus shot may be necessary, so consult a doctor (who will also advise a return visit if there are any signs of infection).

HEAD INJURIES

A blow to the head can result in several kinds of injury. Even though the skull protects the brain very effectively, a head injury can be extremely dangerous, so immediate medical attention is essential.

Cuts to the scalp often bleed heavily, but are rarely serious. If the cut is not the result of a hard blow to the head, apply pressure to stop the bleeding. See a doctor if the cut is very long or deep; it may need stitches.

CONCUSSION

A concussion results from a blow that is strong enough to shake the brain but not to fracture the skull. This can be the result of a blow to the head or to the point of the jaw.

The signs to look for in the victim are
- headache
- paleness
- clammy skin
- nausea
- shallow breathing.

Consciousness may be briefly lost, though not necessarily immediately. Occasionally, the victim may experience a memory loss following a concussion.

A headache lasting for a day or two is the most common symptom of concussion. Most simple concussions heal by themselves with rest. However, any head injury is a serious matter and should be seen by a doctor. The doctor may decide to take X rays of the skull to check for a possible fracture, and may admit the patient to the hospital for observation in case complications develop.

SKULL FRACTURE

Sometimes a blow to the head causes a fracture of the skull. The affected area of the skull can press down onto the tissue of the brain. Compression can develop as long as two days after the victim has apparently recovered from the accident.

With a suspected compression fracture, immediate medical help is essential. The victim will have a flushed face, breathe noisily, and one or both of his pupils will be wide open. The victim will lose consciousness, but not necessarily immediately. Call an ambulance at once.

Sometimes a person receives a blow to the head and does not seem to show any symptoms of injury. Be suspicious—sometimes the symptoms arrive long after the accident. Delayed bleeding within the skull can cause loss of consciousness several hours after the initial accident. Anyone who has had even a brief episode of concussion should be evaluated by a doctor.

Look for:
- traces of blood in the ears, nose, or mouth
- partial paralysis or weakness of the arms and legs on the side opposite the site of the blow
- slurred speech or other disturbance
- headache or dizziness.

If the victim shows any of these signs, even hours or days after the event, you must get medical help at once.

HEART ATTACK

A heart attack occurs when an area of the heart muscle does not receive enough blood. This usually happens when one of the arteries supplying the heart muscle with blood is blocked by arterial disease or by a clot of blood. The severity of heart attacks may vary. In very mild cases the victim is sometimes not even aware that he has suffered an attack.

If the heart attack is serious, the victim will probably feel a sudden, very severe constricting pain in the chest. He will get sweaty and go very pale in the face; he may have blue-colored lips. He may also be nauseous and short of breath. If the attack is very serious, there may be collapse and loss of consciousness.

Call for emergency medical attention, telling the operator that the victim has suffered a heart attack. Lay the victim down in a comfortable position, loosen his clothing and keep reassuring him. If medical help cannot come to you quickly, then bring the victim to the hospital any way you can. Never give the victim food or drink. If you are certain the heart-attack victim has no pulse at all, and if you are qualified to do so, begin heart massage (see "Heart Massage").

One of the normal responses to the onset of a heart attack is anxiety. That's when you can be of great assistance. The calmer your voice and the more you seem in control of the situation, the more assured the victim will feel and the greater the chances of recovery. Runaway anxiety can feed a heart attack, causing the already taxed heart muscle to pump faster.

Constricting pain in the chest, which may spread to the neck or jaw and left arm, can be the forerunner of a heart attack. If a person mentions these pains, get him to a hospital as soon as possible. Chest pain may be a sign of angina pectoris. If the victim has suffered from this before, he may carry prescription medication to control it; he may also wear a medical-alert tag. Check to see if this is the case and then send for medical help.

Your only job when giving first aid to a heart-attack victim is to help keep him calm until trained professionals arrive.

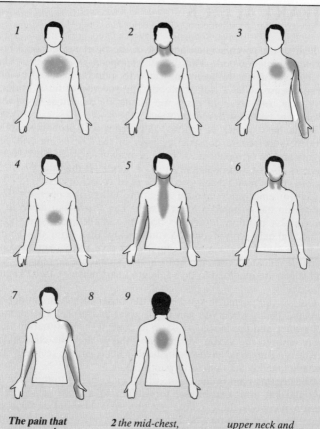

The pain that accompanies a heart attack is usually felt as a sensation of tightness or constriction in the upper chest **1**, but other parts of the body can also be affected, including: **2** the mid-chest, neck and jaw; **3** the mid-chest, left shoulder and left inside arm; **4** the upper abdomen; **5** the central chest area, neck, jaw and inside both arms; **6** both sides of the upper neck and along the jaw from ear to ear; **7 & 8** the inside of the right arm to below the elbow, the left shoulder, inside left arm and hand; and **9** between the shoulder blades.

MYOCARDIAL INFARCTION

The coronary arteries supply the heart muscles with blood and if they are blocked, the area of heart muscle deprived of blood may be more or less seriously damaged.

The symptoms of myocardial infarction commonly include severe centralized chest pain, sweating, loss of color, shortness of breath, nausea and loss of consciousness.

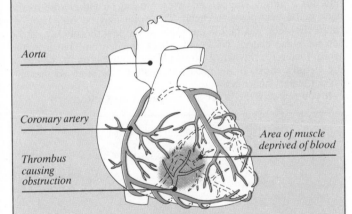

Aorta

Coronary artery

Thrombus causing obstruction

Area of muscle deprived of blood

Myocardial infarction *is another term for a heart attack, used to describe more precisely the damage to heart tissue that occurs when it does not receive sufficient blood. The usual cause is obstruction or narrowing of one of the three main coronary arteries by a fatty substance called atheroma. If the atheroma is laid down on the inner wall of* *an artery, a blod clot, or thrombosis, is a likely outcome, leading to a coronary thrombosis — a term also used for a heart attack. High levels of cholesterol in the blood, cigarette-smoking, diabetes and raised blood pressure have all been implicated as factors that predispose a person to an early heart attack.*

HEART MASSAGE

Heart massage, or cardiopulmonary resuscitation (CPR), can save a life—but it can also be very harmful if done by an unqualified would-be rescuer. The steps are described below for information only. The only rescuers who should ever attempt CPR are those who have been formally trained in the technique at a course taught by a certified professional.

Heart massage should be performed *only* if you are absolutely certain the victim's heart has stopped. A victim who is unconscious may still have a heartbeat.

If you think heart massage may be needed, ensure that the victim is lying on a firm surface—the floor is best—and first check carefully for a pulse. The carotid artery, found on either side of the neck is the best place to check. The pulse may be very faint, so check the neck just below the angle of the jaw thoroughly. If the carotid pulse cannot be found, check the femoral pulse in the groin. Listen for the heartbeat by placing your ear on the center of the victim's chest. If any pulse—no matter how faint—is present, do not start a heart massage.

If you are sure the heart has stopped, start CPR:

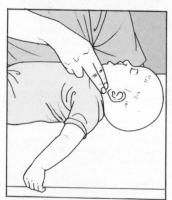 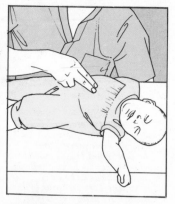

Heart Massage: BABY
1 With the baby on its back on a firm surface, feel for a pulse in the neck as indicated above.

2 Only if there is no pulse, place two fingers on the breastbone and press down firmly — but not too hard — about 80 times a minute.

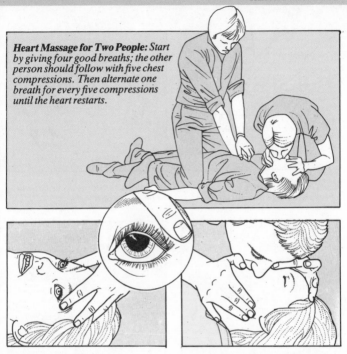

Heart Massage for Two People: *Start by giving four good breaths; the other person should follow with five chest compressions. Then alternate one breath for every five compressions until the heart restarts.*

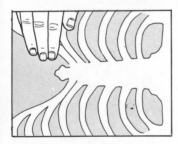

Heart Massage: CHILD
Check pulse and eyes for heartbeat.

If none present, give two breaths in mouth-to-mouth respiration.

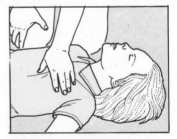

If the heart still does not start beating, begin heart massage in conjunction with artificial respiration. Place the heel of one hand at a point just above the breastbone.

Press the bone down about an inch once every second. After 15 presses give two breaths. Repeat the sequence until the casualty recovers or medical help arrives.

57

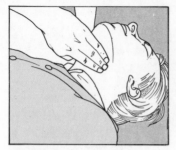

Heart Massage: ADULT
Check the carotid pulse in the neck.

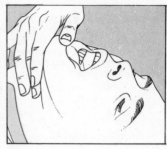

If the heart has stopped, the lips will be bluish in color.

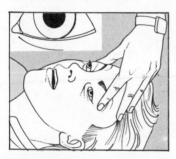

Heart failure is also indicated by dilation of the pupils.

Check the femoral pulse, which is located in the groin.

Listen to the casualty's chest. Begin massage only if you are certain that the heart has stopped.

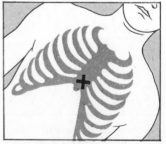

Run your fingers up the inside of the ribcage. The massage point is just above the breastbone.

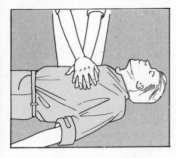

Press down firmly five times at one second intervals.

Pinch the casualty's nose closed, and give one good breath.

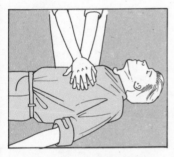

Repeat the compressions a further five times at the same rate.

Give another breath by mouth-to-mouth respiration.

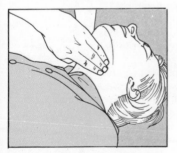

Continue the sequence, checking for a pulse with every breath. Stop massage once the heartbeat resumes.

Even after the heartbeat is restored, it may be necessary to continue artificial respiration if breathing has not returned to normal. When both pulse and breathing are regular, place the casualty in the recovery position and stay with him or her until medical help arrives. Check the casualty periodically in case resuscitation is again required.

HEATSTROKE

Prolonged exposure to the heat of the sun can cause heatstroke (heat prostration). Young children and the elderly are particularly vulnerable. Heatstroke can be very serious, so summon medical help.

The symptoms of heatstroke include a temperature of 104°F (40°C), flushed and dry skin (the victim will not be sweating), vomiting, and sometimes loss of consciousness.

To treat heatstroke, follow these steps:

- Strip the victim and wrap him in a cold, wet sheet to help bring down his body temperature.
- Fan the victim to help cool him.
- If the victim is unconscious, place him in the recovery position (see "Recovery").
- Take the victim's temperature regularly. When it falls, replace the wet sheet with a dry one. Keep checking the temperature in case it starts to rise again.
- Remember to send for medical help.

HYPOTHERMIA (OVEREXPOSURE TO COLD)

Prolonged exposure to low temperatures may lead to a dangerous and progressive drop in body temperature. This condition, known as hypothermia, is especially dangerous to the elderly or very young. As the victim gets progressively worse, stupor, unconsciousness, and even death may occur.

It is not necessary for the outside temperatures to drop below the freezing point for hypothermia to develop. When there are strong winds, hypothermia can occur even if the temperature is fairly mild. The chances of hypothermia are much greater if the victim's clothing is wet.

Scientific evidence has lately pointed up another interesting facet of hypothermia. Those persons who psychologically are determined to survive seem to have a better chance of making it through the ordeal. It is those people who panic who are more likely to have problems.

The symptoms of hypothermia can be far advanced before they are noticed. As the victim's body gets colder, his physical and mental processes slow down. He becomes pale, clumsy, thinks slowly, speaks indistinctly, and gets sleepy. Eventually he becomes unconscious; the breathing and heartbeat are slow and weak. If you suspect the early stages of hypothermia, check the victim's abdomen; if it feels cold, this is a sure sign of hypothermia.

The basic treatment for hypothermia combines the prevention of further heat loss with warming up the body and administering plenty of hot fluids.

A child with hypothermia needs immediate medical attention. In the meantime, you can help by warming the child with your own body heat. Get into bed with the child and snuggle around him, or wrap a blanket around the child and you. The gradual warmth of body-to-body contact will begin to relieve the problem.

To treat an adult you must prevent further heat loss, then gradually restore the body's normal temperature. If the victim is young, place him in a warm bath and give him a warm, sweet drink. Do not do this if the victim is elderly. An older body's system cannot handle a sudden change in temperature. If the victim is elderly, place him in warm surroundings, give him a warm, sweet drink, and wrap him in blankets. Do not give elderly victims hot-water bottles or electric blankets. These may cause the blood to surge away from the vital organs, which could result in heart failure.

Do not give alcohol to any hypothermia victim. Call for medical help if the victim does not respond quickly to the steps above.

FROSTBITE

Frostbite occurs when the skin and tissues of the body freeze. Frostbite generally occurs on fingers, toes, and the face. The frost-bitten area is hard, white, cold, and numb. After it thaws, it becomes swollen, red, and painful.

Prompt treatment should be given to anyone suffering from frostbite. Get the person out of the cold and into someplace warm. Cover the frozen part with blankets or hold it against your body to warm it. It is very important to treat the injured tissues gently. Do not warm them with direct heat, by holding them near a heater, for example. However, hands and feet can be put in warm water. Do not rub the area.

Frostbite is *a serious medical condition requiring instant and effective medical treatment. Young children particularly should always be warmly dressed when outdoors in windy or cold weather.*

INFECTION PREVENTION

Good hygiene *is a first step toward the prevention of infection.*

An infection occurs when the tissues of the body are invaded by harmful microorganisms such as bacteria or viruses. The body's immune system usually prevents an infection from taking hold, but sometimes this doesn't work completely. Most infections are not first-aid situations.

The primary symptom of local infection is inflammation: redness, local heat, pain, swelling. These are caused by the body's efforts to heal itself. More blood circulates through the area to bring infection-fighting white blood cells to it. If the infection is more severe, there may be oozing and pus around the wound. In a severe infection, the victim feels feverish and ill; there may be angry red streaks radiating around the wound. In all but severe infections, the body's natural defenses usually take their course. A severe infection may need antibiotics to heal.

The primary rule for preventing infection is cleanliness. Always try to wash your hands before treating someone. Use sterile bandages; discard the bandage if the sterile seal has been broken. There will be emergency situations where sterility will be hard to come by. In that case, just use the cleanest thing available.

Minor cuts and scrapes should be washed with mild soap and clean water. Deeper wounds should be searched for any fragments of foreign matter, such as bits of wood or glass, that may be trapped in them. If you cannot wash the foreign matter out, try using a sterile cotton swab. An embedded fragment may have to be removed with tweezers. If this is the case, sterilize the tweezers with rubbing alcohol or hold them briefly in a flame. A deeply embedded fragment should be removed by a doctor.

Gently blot the wound dry with a dry, sterile gauze pad. Apply a sterile dressing and tape it in place.

If any sign of serious infection appears, see your doctor.

The microorganisms that cause infectious diseases are spread through the air, physical contact, and contaminated food or drink.

Physical contact may spread the infectious organisms that thrive on the skin and mucous membranes of the body. The organism may be transmitted by direct contact with an infected person or indirectly by contact with infected clothes, towels or utensils. Touching, kissing or sexual intercourse with an infected person increases your chances of catching the disease yourself. Measles, rubella and chickenpox are communicated by physical contact. Sexually transmitted diseases such as herpes, syphilis, gonorrhea and non-specific urethritis are spread primarily via sexual intercourse.

HYGIENE AT HOME

Personal hygiene and cleanliness are far more than conventional social graces — they are a vital part of preventive medicine. The cleaner you keep yourself and your surroundings, and the more care you take in the storage and preparation of what you eat and drink, the more likely you are to enjoy basic good health.

- Keep all rooms and surfaces clean
- Wash regularly and use clean towels
- Store dirty clothes neatly before washing
- Wash yourhands after using the bathroom
- Dispose of kitchen garbage tidily and daily
- Keep kitchen crockery, pots andpans clean
- Eat perishable foods soon after purchase
- Keep drains clear

Air is the primary medium for spreading some diseases of the respiratory tract, such as colds, influenza, tuberculosis and diptheria. The old rhyme "coughs and sneezes spread diseases" is true, because the offending viruses and bacteria are rapidly expelled from the body in tiny droplets. A cough, for instance, expels the air at speeds up to nearly 1,000ft/sec (300m/sec), spraying droplets over people, clothes, surfaces or food. Many types of organisms will die as soon as the droplets dry out, but some remain virulent for a long time. Sneezes shower droplets over a 3- to 4-yard (3- to 4-m) area. Apart from spreading the germs that cause respiratory diseases, they can release Staphylococcus aureus into the air. This bacterium is found in boils and septic wounds.

The mouth is an ideal entry point for infectious organisms. Tiny, virulent bacteria and viruses contaminate food and water, causing food poisoning and diseases such as polio, cholera and dysentery. It is always best to avoid food that has been imperfectly preserved or left to stand for a long time and to avoid drinking untreated water. From the mouth, the organisms responsible for infection pass through the body and into the feces. For this reason you should always wash your hands after visiting the bathroom.

MUSCLE CRAMPS

A cramp is a long and painful muscle contraction. Cramps often occur during or after unaccustomed or vigorous exercise, or after sitting, standing or lying in an uncomfortable position for a long time. While uncomfortable, cramps are not serious and usually go away quickly.

Cramps from vigorous exercise frequently occur after participation in an athletic activity such as running or swimming. Frequently the pain comes on right after the physical exertion has stopped, when the body begins to cool down. At times the muscles may cramp during the activity.

Muscle cramps that occur while a person is swimming are particularly dangerous, and more often than not they are preventable. Jumping into the sea or a swimming pool immediately after a meal, without giving your digestive system time to do its work, is the most common cause of swimmer's cramp. If this happens you face a real risk of being unable to move in the water and of drowning. If you are swimming and you begin to feel a muscle cramp, don't panic but get out of the water as soon as possible!

Muscle cramps, especially in the arms or legs, are often called charley horses.

Cramps from vigorous exercise should be treated as follows:

● Have the victim walk around, keeping the cramped muscle working as much as possible. By walking, more circulation is drawn to the affected area.

● Massage the aching muscle until it relaxes. Stretch the affected muscle as much as possible by straightening it. If the cramp is in the back of the calf, push the heel back away from the thigh. Place one hand on the heel and the other on the toes, and push the toes as far toward the knee as possible.

● Apply a warm compress to the muscle. Heat on the area provides added blood circulation, which should help relieve the cramp.

Don't dive into a swimming pool. play a violent game, or exercise too soon after a meal. Treat cramp by stretching and massaging the affected area.

MUSCLE STRAIN

Strains are injuries where the muscles or their tendons are stretched or torn, usually due to overexertion. Often known as a pulled muscle, a muscle strain can be quite painful and can have a long recovery period. However, a strain is rarely dangerous or permanent. The basic symptoms of muscle strain include a sudden, sharp pain associated with a loss of power in the muscle. A bad strain may swell and even turn black-and-blue. The injured area will feel very tender and sore throughout the period of recovery.

Virtually any muscle in the body may be strained. One common strain involves the muscles of the lower back. Improperly lifting even lightweight articles can strain the back. Always bend your knees and lift with the legs when lifting something.

Muscles that are rarely used are often strained when suddenly called into service. For example, if you walk down the street and step in a slight depression in the sidewalk, your heel can dip down below the toes and land on solid ground, suddenly stretching your calf muscle. Since you rarely use that type of heel-landing movement that muscle in the back of your calf has spent a relatively "unexercised" life. The sharp pain you experience as you limp home is a muscle strain.

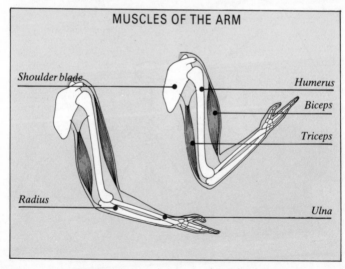

MUSCLES OF THE ARM

Shoulder blade

Humerus

Biceps

Triceps

Radius

Ulna

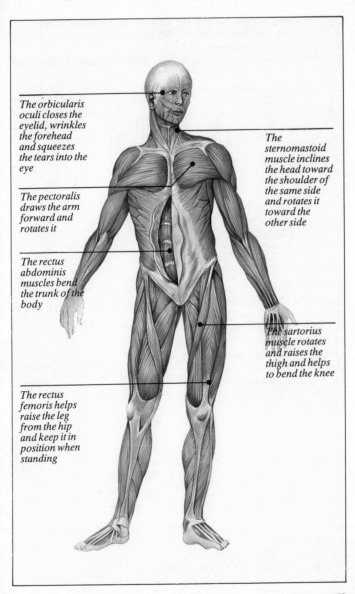

The orbicularis oculi closes the eyelid, wrinkles the forehead and squeezes the tears into the eye

The pectoralis draws the arm forward and rotates it

The rectus abdominis muscles bend the trunk of the body

The sternomastoid muscle inclines the head toward the shoulder of the same side and rotates it toward the other side

The sartorius muscle rotates and raises the thigh and helps to bend the knee

The rectus femoris helps raise the leg from the hip and keep it in position when standing

Certain steps can minimize the damage of a muscle strain:
● Make sure that the victim has no other injury, such as a bone fracture (see "Bone Injuries").
● Gently massage the injured muscle. This will help to relieve the pain.

● Apply an ice pack to the injured area as soon as possible after the injury. Leave it on for about 20 minutes.

● Wrap an elastic bandage snugly (but not too tightly to avoid restricting the blood flow) around the injured area. This compression helps reduce swelling.
● Later, apply heat in the form of hot towels, hot-water bottles, heating pads, or even a hot bath. The heat treatments, following the cold ice pack, help get the muscle to relax and relieve some of the pain.

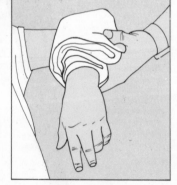

● Rest the injured area, keeping it elevated if possible. If the strain is to the back, placing a stiff board under the mattress gives the victim further support.
● If pain persists, seek medical advice.

NOSEBLEEDS

Nosebleeds are generally caused by damage to the soft tissue lining the inner nose. On rare occasions, nosebleeds may indicate head injuries of a more serious nature, such as skull fractures. If you suspect a serious injury, get immediate medical help.

The causes of nosebleeds are quite numerous. They may occur as the result of a blow to the nose, exposure to high altitudes, nose blowing, excessive dry heat, strenuous activity or even as a side effect of high blood pressure. Like other minor bodily injuries, nosebleeds tend to be more annoying than life-threatening.

Most nosebleeds are nothing more than a rupture of a tiny blood vessel in the nasal cavity. As with any other bleeding situation, the first-aid technique calls for the application of pressure on the wound. In the case of nosebleeds, proper first aid calls for these steps:

● Ask the victim to sit in a chair with the upper body leaning forward. (This may seem strange to some since the old technique called for the head to tilt backward. Most doctors today feel it is better for any excess blood to drain out of the nasal passages, rather than back into the throat.)

● Apply pressure to the nose by pinching the nostrils together for a period of about 8 minutes.

● Keep a small bowl handy to catch any blood. This not only makes the clean-up easier, but reduces the embarrassment for the victim.

● The nosebleed should stop after about 10 minutes. If the bleeding continues, repeat the procedure outlined above and also apply an ice pack to the nose.

● If the bleeding still continues, roll up a sterile gauze pad and insert it into the nostril, leaving part of the pad exposed for easy removal. Do not use cotton balls.

● If this does not work, seek medical help. In cases where nosebleeds occur frequently, a doctor may recommend cauterization of the nasal blood vessels.

Bleeding from both nostrils or from the back of the nose can indicate a serious condition. Get medical help quickly.

POISONING AND ACCIDENTAL DRUG OVERDOSE

Don't let children have access to dangerous chemicals.

Poisoning and accidental drug overdoses are usually the result of swallowing, inhaling, or injecting an injurious agent into the system. Some poisons act directly on the digestive system, others are first absorbed into the body and then act on the nervous system. The ones that attack the nervous system may be more dangerous because the effects are not immediately visible.

In suspected poisoning cases, follow the basic first-aid guidelines below. The best advice calls for you to call for medical help while you begin the procedures.

● If the victim is conscious or the evidence such as a prescription pill bottle is handy, try to identify the drug or poison. When you call for medical help you should tell the person responding what drug or poison has been ingested.

● Wipe any of the drug residue away from the victim's mouth and lips.

● If you find that the substance was a corrosive, such as lye or acid, try to dilute it as much as possible by giving the victim milk or water to drink. Do not force liquids if the victim is unconscious. Do not try to make the victim vomit in cases of corrosive poisoning.

● If the victim is awake and can confirm that the substance wasn't corrosive, push your finger down his throat and make him vomit. Make sure that no vomit is inhaled. Do not administer salt solutions to induce vomiting.

● If the victim is unconscious, place him in the recovery position (see "Recovery"); be prepared to give artificial respiration (see "Artificial Respiration").

If the evidence suggests an accidental drug overdose, it may be difficult to identify the type of drug merely by looking at the victim. Look around the room for vials, bottles or other containers which may hold the drugs. Save these for the doctor. If you suspect that the victim has taken some kind of hallucinogen, take steps to make sure he doesn't injure himself, since his perception will be distorted and he may misjudge distances. Try to keep the victim calm by constant, reassuring conversation.

With both poisoning and accidental drug overdoses you may have to treat the victim for shock (see "Shock"). Watch for the signs of clammy skin and abnormal breathing patterns.

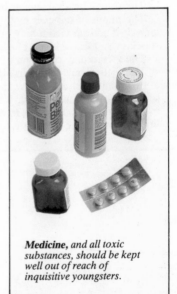

Medicine, and all toxic substances, should be kept well out of reach of inquisitive youngsters.

SHOCK

Shock is an extremely dangerous state caused by a sudden drop in the supply of oxygenated blood to the body. It requires immediate medical attention. In a shock condition, the circulation of the blood is greatly reduced. The drop in circulation may be caused by loss of breathing, heart stoppage, severe injury, loss of blood, severe burns, and other serious medical conditions.

If the victim is in a state of shock, some or all of the following symptoms will be present:

SYMPTOMS
• The complexion will be extremely pale. If the victim is a dark-skinned person, look for a change of color near the fingernails and around the eyes.   • The skin will begin to get moist and clammy.   • Although the pulse will be very rapid, it may be shallow and therefore difficult to feel.   • There may be an irregular breathing pattern.   • The pupils of the eyes may be dilated and appear quite enlarged; if so, the victim may be entering an advanced state of shock.   • The victim may complain of great thirst.   • The victim may complain of nausea.   In potential shock cases, the victim may fall into unconsciousness if left untreated. Keep in mind that some serious injury has caused the shock to begin with. You should treat the injury first, or else all your efforts to control the shock will be useless.

PROCEDURE FOR TREATING SHOCK

● Loosen the victim's clothing. If the clothes don't bind, whatever circulation is present will be able to flow unrestricted.

● If possible, get the victim lying down on his back. Of course, if you suspect an injury to the spine or neck, do not move the victim.

● Raise the victim's legs. Since most of the heart's work consists of pumping blood, elevating the legs makes it easier for the blood to return toward the vital chest and head area. Remember—shock is basically a circulatory problem.

● Keep the victim warm by covering with blankets or coats. Do not use hot-water bottles or a heater.

● Moisten the lips with water, but do not give an actual drink.

● Never give the victim alcohol.

● Keep a constant check on breathing and pulse. If necessary, resort to artificial respiration (see "Artificial Respiration").

● If the victim is conscious, try to keep him calm with reassuring conversation.

● Get medical help as soon as possible.

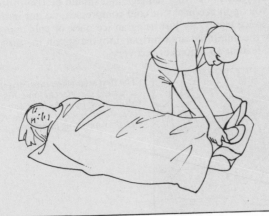

SPRAINS

A sprain is the result of tearing or over-stretching one or more of the ligaments surrounding or supporting a joint. Commonly caused by a violent movement that forces a joint beyond its normal flexibility, a sprain can be quite painful. Besides the pain, the joint cannot support weight or be moved, and generally becomes swollen. After the swelling subsides, a bruise may appear.

One problem in treating sprains is that the sprained area may surround a bone fracture. With this in mind, your first-aid steps will allow you to give support to both the sprain and any potential facture:

● Lay the victim down gently. Remember, you must consider the possibility of fracture and any movement of the bone can be harmful. If the ankle or knee is sprained, do not allow the victim to walk on it.

● Raise the affected joint to help reduce swelling.

● Remove any clothing covering the joint. Apply an ice pack or cold compress (if available) for about 20 minutes.

● Try to keep the strained area immobile. It might be necessary to apply a splint or bandage (see "Bones").

● If the sprain seems serious or there is any possibility of a fracture, the victim should get medical attention.

It is vital that you never apply heat to the sprain. Heat will only induce swelling by opening up the blood vessels in the injured area. Swelling may lead to further damage and should be controlled.

When you apply ice packs or cold compresses, do not immerse the joint in ice water. By just using an ice pack or cold compress you allow the uninjured area surrounding the sprain to "breathe" normally, leading to a quicker recovery.

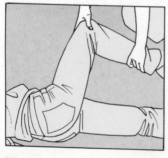

The first step when treating a sprain is to raise the affected joint. Remove all clothing from the joint and apply cold water or ice, if available. Apply a tight supporting bandage.

TOOTHACHES AND TOOTH INJURIES

Toothaches happen when decay in the enamel of a tooth causes a small cavity. If this is not treated by a dentist, the cavity gets larger until it affects the nerves in the pulp of the tooth, causing a toothache. In addition to severe pain, other symptoms of a toothache include: swelling, redness in the area of the tooth, and sensitivity to sweets, heat, and cold. An abscess may form around the root of the tooth. This can lead to severe pain and swelling in the jaw and gum, as well as a fever. An aching tooth, especially if it may be abscessed, needs to be treated by a dentist as soon as possible. If the tooth if not treated promptly, it may be lost. In the meantime, aspirin may help relieve some of the pain and swelling. Rinsing the mouth every hour or so with warm salt water may also help.

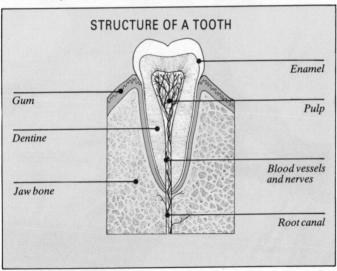

STRUCTURE OF A TOOTH

Enamel

Gum

Pulp

Dentine

Blood vessels and nerves

Jaw bone

Root canal

A blow to the mouth can chip or break a tooth, or even knock a tooth out of its socket. A dentist should be seen immediately. A tooth that has been knocked out can sometimes be reimplanted. If you can find the tooth, place it in a clean plastic bag; then place the bag into another plastic bag filled with ice and bring it along with you to the dentist. If no ice is available, simply place the tooth into a clean container.

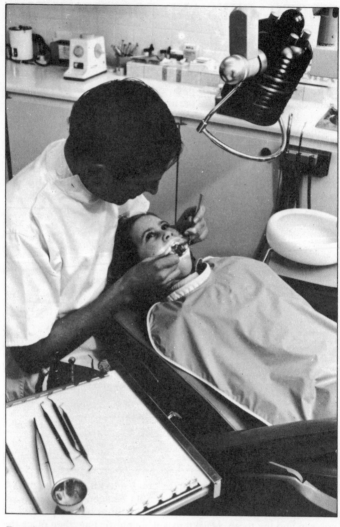

Even though milk teeth are eventually lost, sound dental hygiene at an early age, coupled with regular visits to the dentist, are important in order to lay the foundation for healthy teeth later on in life.

CARIES

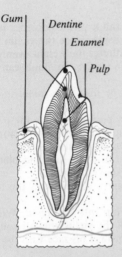

Gum | Dentine | Enamel | Pulp

A healthy tooth has an unbroken layer of dentine protecting dentine and pulp.

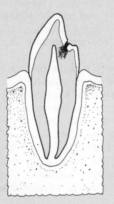

Caries begin when acid, formed from bacteria by food, erodes a cavity.

Decay spreads through the dentine, allowing bacteria to infect the pulp.

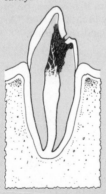

Inflammation sets in, pressing on nerves and causing toothache.

RECOVERY

After you have done everything you can to give emergency help to a victim and are waiting for help to come, place the victim in the recovery position. This position distributes the weight evenly over the body and lets the victim breathe freely; any fluids can drain easily from the mouth.

The recovery position should not be used if a spinal injury is suspected.

To move a victim into the recovery position, follow these steps:

● If the victim is unconscious, be sure he is breathing normally (see "Artificial Respiration"). Loosen any tight clothing.

● Place the victim on his back. Kneel at his side and place the nearest arm and hand straight back above his head.

● Cross the other arm over the victim's chest. Cross the far leg over the near leg at the knee.

● Hold the victim's clothing at the hip with one hand. With the other, support the head. Gently pull the victim toward you from the hip; turn the victim's head and protect his face with the other hand.

● Gently move the upper arm and thigh of one side, bending them at the elbow and knee until they form right angles with the body.

● Tilt the head back and pull the chin forward and down. Cover the victim if possible; be prepared to help if the victim develops difficulty breathing (see "Artificial Respiration"). Stay nearby and be calm and reassuring.

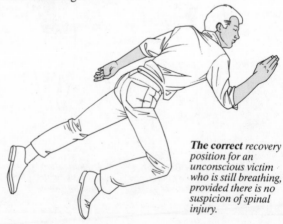

The correct recovery position for an unconscious victim who is still breathing, provided there is no suspicion of spinal injury.

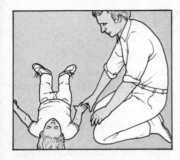

Putting a child into the recovery position: 1 *Loosen clothing.*

2 Place nearest arm under the buttocks. Place other arm on chest.

3 Cross the leg farthest away from you over the other leg.

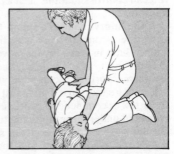

4 Roll the child toward you and support him against your knees.

5 Bend top leg at knee. Place top arm beside head. Pull other arm out.

6 Carefully lift the head up and back to aid breathing.

EMERGENCY TRANSFERS

There are essentially two types of emergency transfers. One involves the necessity of moving a victim to a place of safety and away from the site of the accident. The other transfer is when you must bring the victim to medical attention.

When you have to move the victim for safety reasons, you must do so quickly but without moving any body parts if at all possible. Follow these first-aid procedures:

● If you have the time, check the victim for injuries. Sometimes, despite the danger of the location (for example, a busy highway), first-aid measures such as artificial respiration must be applied. If you can control situations such as bleeding, then you can begin the transport.

● If the injury requires a splint, try to do so before attempting to move the victim. If there isn't time for a splint, try to hold the injured limb in place as you move the victim.

● If the injury is to the head, back, or pelvis (hip area) you must try to transport the victim in a lying-down position.

If you are by yourself and must transport the victim alone, there are a few recommended procedures. If you must pull the victim, grab hold under the armpits and tug the victim along a straight line. Do not push or pull the victim sideways. Take advantage of the body's natural lines and pull the victim in line with the spine. Pulling the victim can be made easier if you can insert a blanket underneath him. The blanket reduces friction and makes movement less of a strain. If a blanket isn't available, use a piece of cardboard or even your shirt.

If you feel that you can lift the person, and if the injury is not to the head, spine, or pelvic region, place one hand under the victim's knees and the other around the waist. Bend your knees, grasp the victim and, pushing up with your legs, lift the victim. This way you not only have a secure hold of the victim, but you reduce the likelihood that you'll strain your back.

If the victim's injury is such that he is still able to walk with some assistance, stand next to the victim and place his nearest arm around your shoulders. Hold him around the waist with your nearest arm to assist his movements. If the injury is to the leg, stand on the same side as the injury.

If there is someone else available, place the victim between the two of you, with his arms around your shoulders.

Sometimes the victim is injured in a chair and unable to move.

Actually, this will make any transfer easier. Get another person to help you as you take the front feet of the chair and your assistant holds the chair's back. Tilt the chair and victim back and then lift the chair. Carry the victim to safety or medical attention.

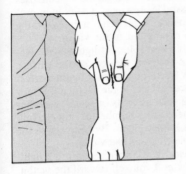

To stop bleeding *from an open superficial wound apply direct local pressure by holding the edges of the wound firmly together until the bleeding stops and a clot forms.*

Leg injuries *commonly require a splint. Move the damaged limb gently against the other one.*

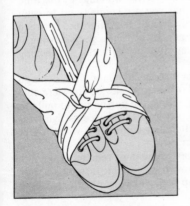

Place firm padding *between knees and ankles and secure the legs together with adequate bandages, at different points down the leg avoiding the site of the injury.*

Improvise a splint *which must reach from crotch to foot. Lay the splint against the leg and secure it, and the padding, with the bandages.*

ICE RESCUE

One of the more dangerous rescues is one attempted over ice. Frequently the rescuer becomes another victim as the ice collapses beneath the attempt. For a successful ice rescue you need to improvise. Before venturing out onto the ice, see if you can find anything that you might be able to use to extend out to the victim.

Useful devices should be readily movable and lightweight. Remember that someone has fallen through the ice, so the surface should be treated with respect. A tree limb that may be the perfect length may be too heavy for the ice surface. Some useful items may include rope, poles, and clothing such as coats or scarfs. Another useful item is other people. If there are a number of others available, get them to help you form a human chain. By lying across the ice ankle to arm, you may be able to reach the victim.

Perhaps the best reaching device is a ladder because it's lightweight and allows you to safely extend yourself toward the victim. The only drawback is that usually a ladder is not quickly found.

When venturing out onto the ice you must distribute your body weight evenly. Assuming that the ice is thin in some spots, the trick here is to get on your stomach and almost crawl to the victim. As you crawl along the ice, call out to the victim, who may by this time begin to panic. Tell the victim that you are coming and to calm down. Reducing the victim's panic may be the difference between being able to make the rescue or not. If the victim starts clawing at the ice, his frantic actions may cause the ice to break up, sending you into the water.

If the ice near where the victim is seems to be too thin, don't go any closer. Take hold of one end of whatever device you were able to find. Toss it toward the victim, telling the person not to pull too hard. Ideally, the victim should just hold the device as tightly as possible while you pull him out. Tell the victim to kick with the feet to help ease him out of the water.

Once the victim is out of the water, you must remember the thin ice beneath you. Do not huddle with the victim. Instead keep on your stomach, instruct the victim to do likewise, and crawl back toward shore.

After you've reached the shore, keep the victim as warm as possible and try to get him a change of clothes. Look for signs of exposure (see "Hypothermia") and treat if necessary. Get the victim to a doctor as soon as possible if he has been injured or does not respond to treatment for hypothermia.

TRAVEL FIRST-AID KIT

The last thing you need on a vacation or business trip is to suffer some injury and be ill-prepared to take care of it. It's a good idea to pack a few first-aid essentials in your bag. Your kit should include:

● Several bandages of assorted sizes.

● Everything you need to treat a blister (see "Blisters"). A common problem while traveling is blisters, especially if you're sight-seeing. Keep an eye on the blister for signs of infection.

● Aspirin or acetaminophen tablets for relief of simple headache, muscle pain and fever.

● Prescription drugs. If you are taking any prescription drugs it's a good idea to pack them in a convenient place, like your travel first-aid kit. Prescriptions may be difficult to refill on the road, so make sure you have enough medication even if you extend your stay.

● If you are going to an insect-ridden area, take along some repellent and some calamine lotion.

● Unfortunately, a common problem while traveling is diarrhea. Since the body becomes used to particular region's water, any change might affect the digestive system. Take along a bottle of over-the-counter liquid medication for diarrhea to combat the attacks.

● If you are going camping, put an auxiliary flashlight with fresh batteries in your first-aid kit. You can never have too many flashlights on a camping trip.

Another thing to remember while on a trip is that your entire system is accustomed to living a certain way. If you are normally a sensible eater, don't go wild just because you're on a vacation or business trip. If you're on a restricted sodium or cholesterol diet, a vacation isn't a signal to load up on those juicy steaks and french fries!

SAFETY AT HOME

Most accidents happen in the home; many are preventable. Safety in the home is one of the most important elements of preventive medicine. By taking simple precautions and actions, you can minimize the risk of household accidents and injuries, particularly to babies and young children.

CHILD SAFETY

Some extra precautions for homes with small children should include:

● Keep plastic bags out of reach. Children can suffocate if they pull such bags over their heads.

● Keep small items such as buttons and coins out of reach of small hands. These items resemble candy to children and may be swallowed and cause choking.

● Always place kettles, pots and so on on the back burners of the stove, away from a child's reach, make sure handles are turned inward. Along the same lines, never drink anything hot while a child is sitting on your lap.

● Never let tablecloths extend over the edges of tables, in case a child pulls at them.

● Never leave a baby or child alone in a bath.

● Make sure all windows are fitted with child-proof safety catches. In addition, you should keep balcony doors locked.

● Keep all medicines out of reach and always lock your medicine cabinet. Medicine looks like candy!

● Flush old medicines down the toilet.

● Never use old bottles to store poisonous fluids.

● Keep lighters and matches out of reach.

● Never buy toys with sharp, pointed edges.

● Keep knives and other sharp objects and tools out of reach.

● Never let your child cross the street alone. Make sure your child understands bicycle safety and that the bicycle is properly maintained.

● In the car, make sure the children have their seat belts buckled. A baby should always travel in a special baby seat in the back seat.

● Electricity poses special problems for children. Instruct the children about the dangers of electricity. Make sure your wiring is in good condition and that plugs are properly connected. Use outlet guards to avoid the chance of a child poking a finger into an outlet.

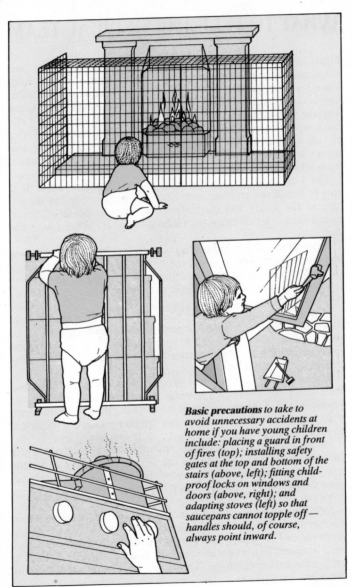

Basic precautions to take to avoid unnecessary accidents at home if you have young children include: placing a guard in front of fires (top); installing safety gates at the top and bottom of the stairs (above, left); fitting child-proof locks on windows and doors (above, right); and adapting stoves (left) so that saucepans cannot topple off — handles should, of course, always point inward.

WHAT TO TELL THE MEDICAL TEAM

Either before or just after you've completed your emergency first-aid it may well be necessary for you to telephone medical help. Since you've tried to control the situation concerning the victim, now is not the time to panic. Your role as a life-saver doesn't stop with the first-aid treatment. All your efforts could be in vain if you can't explain the problem clearly to the medical personnel. Above all, continue to stay calm, try to think logically and clearly, and work out exactly what you want to tell the members of the medical team when they arrive.

The first thing you should relay is what has happened. It is always best if the arriving ambulance has been notified of the nature of the injury and can prepare a better response—a heart-rescue alert is far different than a broken leg. Be as specific as you can.

If, for example, you are dealing with an accidental drug overdose and you've been able to locate the type of drug, be sure to convey that information. This way the arriving medical team can continue treating the victim at once without delaying at the scene to ask you what happened.

Of course, you must describe where the victim is located. People sometimes are in such a rush to get help that they forget to give an exact address or location. Be as specific as you can. If the victim, for example, is lying in the stairwell of the building, don't send the arriving team to the basement.

It may be necessary for the rescue team to locate you after they have taken the victim to a hospital. Sometimes they may need to know what first-aid you performed and when. Be sure to give them your name and tell them where you can be contacted if they need to speak to you.

As a further help to the rescue team ask if there is anything else that you could or should do for the victim while you wait for the ambulance to arrive. There may be times when you can give additional help that could make the victim more comfortable or aid in recovery.

Since the response person is certain to be more accustomed than you are to dealing with medical emergencies, it's highly likely that he or she will be able to help you and remind you of something you may have neglected. As an amateur, you cannot be expected to remember to do everything. The simple rule is not to hang up until the other party does.

WHEN YOU'RE HURT AND ALONE

First aid is just not something that you apply to other people. There may be times in your life when you are injured, alone, and must treat yourself. The first thing to remember is not to panic. This is a time when a clear head may keep you alive! If you begin to panic, and you just might do so because it's always harder to see your own injury than someone else's, try talking to yourself. Be self-assuring. You've read this book . . . you're on top of the problem.

Give yourself a quick examination and try to decide exactly what's wrong. Be thorough, but be quick. If the injury is one that may trigger other problems, like respiratory failure, you must act fast to control it. It's impossible to give artificial respiration to yourself!

Next, see if you can treat the injury. Remember that your purpose now is not to make yourself well, but to patch things up enough so that you can get to a telephone or to the hospital. If you cannot move, try to come up with some method to attract attention. Is there a fire alarm that you can trigger? Try shouting or banging against the walls. Don't be embarrassed—make as much noise as you can!

Whether you get help or not, try to apply some first aid to your injury. If you begin to feel sweaty, cover yourself up to prevent shock. If a limb is injured, try to raise it to reduce swelling. Always make sure that you minimize blood loss by holding an injured limb high, by covering a wound and by pressing on a pressure point nearby the wound to reduce the bleeding. It is also important to keep warm and, above all, to think positively.

You may have to improvise, so use your head and be creative. Since most of us don't walk around with tape and dressings, you may have to tear off a piece of your clothing to make a bandage. Don't worry too much about the possibility of infection now. Even if it isn't sterilized, a shirt sleeve may do wonders to stop the bleeding. When you're able to get to the hospital, they can treat the cut properly.

If you have been able to telephone for help, then try to make yourself comfortable after giving yourself what first aid you can. If you're at home, unlock the door (the rescue team can't help you if they can't get in) and lie down. Telephone a friend or relative and ask them either to come over or meet you at the hospital.

ESCAPE FROM FIRE

A home fire can be very destructive in a very short time. To prevent serious injuries or even death from a fire, families should plan ahead. Install smoke detectors and check the batteries often. Sit down with your family and devise a step-by-step procedure for evacuating the house in case of fire. Draw a sketch of every room in the house and discuss ways of escape. The more the family gets involved in the planning, the easier it'll be to leave the burning home. Designate somebody as fire marshal. That person's job will be to make sure everybody is out of the house and then to call the fire department.

If you have children, get them involved by making them junior fire marshals. Instruct them about fire hazards and have them search the house for potential problems.

If your home has a fire, your chances of escaping uninjured are better if you remember these rules:

- Since hot air rises, you should drop near the floor when vacating

the house. Cover your mouth and nose with a dampened cloth if possible.

If your clothes catch on fire, don't panic. Roll around on the floor to put them out. If someone's else's clothes are burning, try to smother the flames with a blanket or push them to the ground and roll them around.

When escaping, be careful with closed doors. Before opening a door, put your palm against it to feel for heat. If the door is hot, leave by another exit. If the door feels cold, open it slightly. Pass your hand into the other room. If the room air feels cool, you may enter.

When leaving a room, close the door behind you. The less air that circulates around the house, the less the fire will be fanned.

If you live in a tall building try to hang a sheet out the window to signal potential rescuers of your location.

After escaping check your family for any signs of smoke inhalation. See if anybody is having trouble breathing; if so start giving artificial respiration. Fire department personnel are trained in emergency procedures. Don't be afraid to ask them for help.

HOME FIRST-AID KIT

In order to cope with the day-to-day responsibilities of first aid, every home should have a properly equipped first-aid kit. While bandages and dressings can be improvised in an emergency, it is far better to have everything that you might need on hand.

Although it's convenient to have a portable kit, it's also advisable to have a well-stocked medicine cabinet. The contents should include: aspirin, acetaminophen, an antihistamine/antiseptic cream for insect bites and stings, antacid for indigestion, calamine lotion to soothe sunburn, insect bites and minor skin irritations, and some petroleum jelly.

1 cotton balls
2 elastic bandage
   and butterfly closures
3 stretch gauze bandage
4 gauze swabs
5 antacid
6 Epsom salts
7 calamine lotion
8 aspirin
9 children's aspirin
10 acetaminophen
11 salt tablets
12 adhesive tape
13 assorted adhesive bandages
14 sterile pads for bandaging
15 sharp blunt-ended scissors
16 lipscreen
17 cotton swabs
18 petroleum jelly
19 analgesic tablets
20 antacid tablets
21 antibiotic ointment
22 set measuring spoons
23 tweezers
24 family thermometers

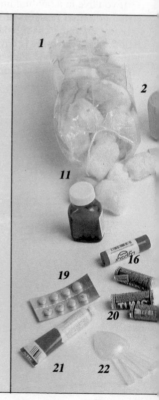

Besides all the medicines it's a good idea to keep this book in the first-aid kit or medicine chest. Although you've read its contents, you may want to check on a few procedures.

The contents of your first-aid kit and medicine cabinet should always be kept out of the reach of children. Dressings, for instance, are useless if not sterile. Medicines can be harmful if swallowed at random. Always buy medicine in bottles with childproof tops. If you have finished a recommended course of prescribed medication and there is still some left, dispose of it. Note the expiration dates of over-the-counter medications on the side of the container. Medicines can begin to break down chemically and you shouldn't use "old" medicine. Consult your doctor or pharmacist for proper storage and disposal.

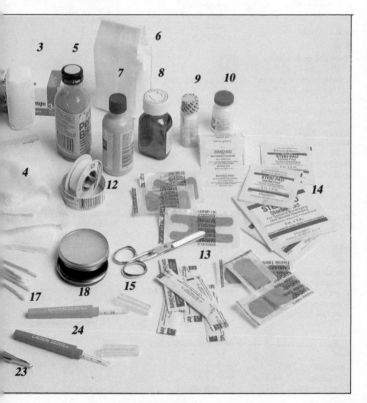

INDEX

Page numbers in *italic* refer to the illustrations and captions

EMERGENCY NUMBERS

Post a copy of this list of emergency phone numbers near every phone in your house.

Police	
Fire Department	
Rescue Squad or Ambulance	
Hospital Emergency	
Poison Control Center	
Health Department	
Pediatrician	Home
Family Doctor	Home
Alternative Doctor	Home
Dentist	Home
All-Night Drugstore	
Father's Work Number	
Mother's Work Number	
Neighbors	
Taxi	

Credits:

Art Director: Peter Bridgewater
Editorial Consultants: Maria Pal/Clark Robinson Ltd

Picture credits:

The author and publishers have made every effort to identify the
copyright owners of the photographs; they apologize for any
omissions and wish to thank the following:

Geoff Banks, 91; Sheila Buff, 67; Mick Hill, 23; Alex Williams,
43; John Heseltine, 92–93; John Watney, 63, 72, 78; Trevor
Wood, 62.